Blessings as you catch glimpses of Gods presence in your life.

Duane Ulleland

Dec. 2008

Glimpses

of

God's Presence

REFLECTIONS ON GRACE, FAITH, HOPE, LOVE AND PRAYER

DUANE ULLELAND

Copyright © 2008 Duane Ulleland
All rights reserved.

ISBN: 1-4392-0764-X
ISBN-13: 9781439207642

Visit www.booksurge.com to order additional copies.

Scripture quotations are from New Revised Standard Version Bible,
copyright 1989, Division of Christian Education of the National
Council of the Churches of Christ in the United States of America.
Used by permission. All rights reseved.

CONTENTS

Preface
7

In Daily Life
9

In Living and Growing as a Christian
23

In Prayer
69

In Our Scattered Thoughts
93

In Grace and Forgiveness
163

In Faith, Hope, and Love
191

In Special Days
219

To
Marilyn
my wonderful wife
a loving companion on life's journey
an encourager and supporter in ministry

PREFACE

God certainly has interesting ways of leading us along unexpected pathways in the journey of life.

If anyone had predicted at the time of my retirement that I would be engaged in a writing ministry within three years, I would have insisted that person was out of touch with reality. After forty years as a parish pastor and nursing home chaplain, I felt I had done more than enough writing. Retirement was to be a time to do something different.

Two years into retirement I was asked to do a seven-month interim ministry at St. John's Lutheran Church in Medical Lake, WA (another thing I had vowed I would not do). A month into that ministry I received an advertisement for an e-mail daily devotional service to which congregations were invited to subscribe. I did not subscribe to the service, but I was motivated to try writing some inspirational thoughts which would reach out to families of the church between Sundays. When I requested e-mail addresses at the next worship service, ten or twelve of them showed up in the offering plates. So on June 25, 1999, I sent out some reflections on the journeys of the Monarch butterflies. During the following months I continued to write brief messages three or four times a week.

By the time I completed my interim assignment people had begun telling others about the messages, and forwarding them to their friends. My mailing list had begun to grow. Many requested that I not stop writing and sending the messages to them, even though the interim would come to an end. Out of that parish ministry experience it seemed that the Lord was calling me to a new writing ministry. Through word of mouth (or perhaps word of e-mail) the mailing list continued to grow until it has included people in many parts of the United States and in a dozen foreign countries. Several recipients have requested that I publish the messages, and so this book is being offered.

Thanks to the people of St. John's who helped launch this ministry, and to many recipients of the e-mails who have spontaneously encouraged me to publish a collection of them. Thanks to my sister-in-law, Carol Buchanan, who has provided encouragement, information and assistance in the publishing process, and to Claudia Schorzman who graciously offered her expertise as an English teacher to significantly improve the quality of the manuscript. I appreciate the assistance of the BookSurge staff who helped guide me through the procedures of publishing. A huge debt of gratitude is due to my wife, Marilyn, who has been an encourager and supporter in this ministry as well as throughout all the years of ministry we have shared. She has frequently proposed ideas for these reflections and regularly read and suggested improvements. But most of all, thanks to God who has equipped me for this work, called a reluctant servant to it, and guided me in it. The credit and honor belong to God.

God's Presence In Daily Life

IN DAILY LIFE

Signs of God's Presence

*My eyes have seen your salvation, which you have
prepared in the presence of all peoples.*

Luke 2:30

It was a beautiful October evening as Marilyn and I were enjoying
a visit at the home of some friends. The four of us were watching
the changing colors as the sun was painting orange clouds against
the background of a pale blue sky. It appeared that someone was
drawing a straight colored line across the face of the clouds and
sky. The line was gradually getting longer. Though we could not
see it, we knew it was an airplane leaving its contrail.

We began talking about how the presence of God in our lives is
something like that airplane. We cannot see him, but we can see
the signs of his presence if we will but look.

We can see the signs in the beauty and variety of his creation. What
an imagination God has! And yes, there are even suggestions of
his humor in his creation. We can see signs in people whose lives
have been touched, changed, shaped through the Spirit of Jesus-
people striving to be loyal followers of Jesus. We can see signs in
the Word and the Sacraments. We are blessed as we recognize the
signs.

God bless you as you see the signs of his loving presence around
you today.

11

GLIMPSES OF GOD'S PRESENCE

I Spy

Blessed are your eyes, for they see, and your ears, for they hear.

Matthew 13:16

When her children were young, Amy would regularly play "I spy" with them, asking where they had seen God during the day. She would also share with them how she had seen God. Sometimes it might be in the beauty of a sunset, or the new fallen snow. Another day it might be in the way a child's fingers moved, or in some circumstance where it seemed God had guided or protected them. The children grew up sensing the presence of God in their lives much more than most children, simply because they were looking for the signs of his presence.

Often what we see depends on what we are looking for. I am reminded of a friend who, on several occasions when we were riding together in a vehicle, would say, "Look, there's a coyote." I suspect that he spotted them when I didn't, partially because his vision was sharper than mine, but mostly because he was looking for them and I wasn't. Often when he pointed them out, I would see them. It makes me wonder how much more I would notice the signs of God's presence if I were more diligent in looking for them.

Blessings as you play "I spy" today.

IN DAILY LIFE

When God Approaches Quietly

Now there was a great wind, so strong that it was splitting mountains and breaking rocks in pieces before the Lord, but the Lord was not in the wind; and after the wind...a sound of sheer silence....Then there came a voice to him that said, "What are you doing here, Elijah?"
I Kings 19:11-13

Naaman, the respected and powerful army commander, felt he had just been snubbed by Elisha, who would not even come out of his house to talk with him. Having been told that Elisha could heal his leprosy, Naaman approached Elisha's house bringing splendid gifts to pay for the expected miracle. Instead of dramatically healing the commander, the prophet merely sent his servant out to tell the commander to go and wash seven times in the river Jordan. Naaman went away in a rage. It was only when his servant urged him to try the seven washings that he was healed.

Do you know people like Naaman, upset with God if he doesn't act in the ways they expect? "If only God would _____, then I could believe in him."

Typically God comes in quiet, unspectacular ways to call us to faith. He came as a baby born to a humble woman on the lower end of the prestige scale. He comes today through words which tell us of his incomprehensible love through Jesus. Through the simple water of baptism he grafts us into Jesus. In bread and wine he nourishes our faith. As we are receptive to him in the ways he chooses to approach us, we can experience his healing power for our lives.

Blessings as you listen for the quiet voice of God.

The Blossom

When the fullness of time had come, God sent his Son...so that we might receive adoption as children.

Galatians 4:4, 5

A beautiful, light blue clematis blossom, fringed with new fallen snow, was just barely visible from our kitchen window. It was almost hidden by the dead leaves still clinging to the vine. Logic says the clematis should not have been blooming-not with the leaves long gone from the deciduous trees, a thick blanket of snow on the ground, and the frost having brought the demise of summer's flowers. Almost miraculously, the blossom peeked out at us, mocking the season.

The blossom is a reminder to me of how God can appear in the most unlikely times and places to bring his grace into our lives. The straw of Bethlehem's stable and Calvary's cross during the harsh Roman occupation were not places anyone expected to catch a glimpse of God's grace and love. Yet it was precisely in those places that the mystery and the beauty of God's love has been revealed to us.

Many of us experience a "winter of the soul," a time of spiritual and emotional barrenness, when we are covered by a blanket of stress and God seems hidden behind clouds of gloom. In those times we can remember God's promise never to fail us or forsake us. The cross of Jesus and his empty tomb are the assurance that the plant of his love is always alive and that, while sometimes obscured, the blossoms are there, waiting to be revealed to us through his channels of grace.

Blessings as the blossom appears for you.

IN DAILY LIFE

The Center of the Circle

Draw near to God, and he will draw near to you.
James 4:8

During my year of internship the high school youth group scheduled a program titled "Youth Asks the Pastor," which was an opportunity for the young people to ask my supervising pastor all kinds of questions about faith and life. After several behavior oriented questions about whether it was all right for a Christian to participate in certain activities, the pastor asked the young people to imagine a large circle with Jesus standing in the very center of the circle. Then he commented that the questions they were asking had a common theme: could they behave in some specific way and still be in the circle? Instead of wondering how close they could get to the edge of the circle without actually going outside, he challenged them to consider behavior patterns which drew them as close as possible to the center of the circle, where Jesus is.

In daily living there are many tugs toward the outside of the circle negatively impacting our spiritual life. Thankfully, God does not turn his back on us, but continually pulls us toward the center where we hear the voice of the One who said, "I came that they may have life, and have it abundantly" (John 10:10).

To counter the tugs toward the outside, it is important that we frequently find ways to move toward the center of the circle. What are some ways you have found to help you do that? Put those behaviors into practice. You may find it helpful to ask Christian friends about what has helped draw them nearer to Christ. That could lead to some interesting discussions.

Blessings as you are drawn to the center.

15

GLIMPSES OF GOD'S PRESENCE

The Quiet Place

(Jesus) said to them, "Come away to a deserted place all by yourselves and rest a while."

Mark 6:31

Walking the sidewalks of Manhattan is a different experience for one who is more accustomed to the open spaces of the eastern side of the state of Washington. I'm sure many identified Marilyn and me as tourists as we gawked at the tall buildings which made the streets like canyons. We were careful about our rubbernecking, though, lest we be run over by the constant swarm of pedestrians coming toward us.

For us the most significant part of the day was the time we spent in the Cathedral of St. Patrick, a beautiful Gothic edifice whose vaulted ceiling lifted our hearts in praise. We sat for some time in row 104, a quiet spot seemingly far removed from the hubbub and sounds of traffic and people just outside the doors of the magnificent building. There was a constant movement of people up and down the central aisle as they quietly went to find a place to sit and meditate, and then left again in silence. There was a wonderful atmosphere of reverence despite all the people. We were moved to prayers and tears as we felt the presence of God in that beautiful, quiet place. St. Patrick's gave us something Macy's and the Empire State Building could never offer.

The experience reminded me of the importance of finding quiet, refreshing times in the presence of God in the midst of our often hectic lives. It is difficult to carve out the quiet time. But when we do, God is likely to surprise us with a renewal of spirit, as he did for Marilyn and me in St. Patrick's.

Blessings in your quiet moments with God.

IN DAILY LIFE

Recognition

*I am the good shepherd. I know my own and my
own know me.*

John 10:14

He came up to me in the grocery store and started talking to me
as if I were a long lost friend. I could not connect him to a time or
place. I was hoping that there would be some clue in what he said
to identify him. The years without contact had simply blurred my
memory.

In the story in John 10: 22-30 Jesus had an encounter with some of
the religious leaders who did not realize he was the Messiah. They,
of all people, should have recognized him. Jesus commented that
they did not believe in him because they were not of his sheep,
but "My sheep hear my voice, and I know them, and they follow
me." It is interesting to note that those who heard his voice and
followed him were not generally among those considered to be
the "religious people."

Our Christian faith affirms that God meets us in the events and
persons we encounter each day. How can we recognize his
presence? The man in the grocery store gives a hint. I struggled
to identify him because there had been no contact with him
for several years. I am convinced that we will be able to know
the presence of God and that our lives will be enriched by the
awareness of his presence, if we are putting ourselves in the places
where the relationship with him will be nurtured. The sheep who
heard Jesus' voice rejoiced in his presence, and followed him were
the ones who had been spending time with him.

Blessings as you recognize the presence of the Living Lord in your
life today.

GLIMPSES OF GOD'S PRESENCE

The Voice of God

*The Word became flesh and lived among us, and
we have seen his glory, the glory as of the Father's
only Son, full of grace and truth.*

John 1:14

As I was reading Psalm 29 I was struck by the description of how God speaks. In part it reads: "The voice of the Lord is over the waters; the God of glory thunders, the Lord, over mighty waters. The voice of the Lord is powerful, the voice of the Lord is full of majesty." Then the Psalmist says that the voice of the Lord:

...breaks the cedars, ...flashes forth flames of fire ...shakes the wilderness ...causes the oaks to whirl ...strips the forests bare.

These results of God speaking reminds me of the time Mt. St. Helens erupted, and more than three inches of volcanic ash were dumped on us in Ritzville, WA, more than 200 miles from the volcano. Several times in the ensuing days I heard the comment, "God must be trying to tell us something." It's a terrifying voice of God which comes in that way.

At Christmas God's voice came to us in a different way: through an infant in a manger. John tells us that Jesus is the Word of God in human flesh. It is a word of love, forgiveness, mercy and grace which comes through Jesus. It's a word which tells us, "You are my beloved child." This voice does not leave us terrified. But it does leave us with a question: "How can I express my gratitude for such gracious love and acceptance?

Blessings as you joyfully answer that question today.

IN DAILY LIFE

Rearranging the Furniture

For everything there is a season, and a time for every matter under heaven...a time to keep, and a time to throw away.

Ecclesiastes 3:1, 6

The purchase of a recliner rocker turned out to be more of an endeavor than we anticipated. We knew where we wanted to place the chair, but that involved moving three other chairs, a book case (twice), and finding new locations for eight pictures (and of course, patching nail holes). We did not dream that one chair would end up in such a rearrangement of the house, but we are pleased with the result.

Many have discovered that a similar rearrangement of the furniture of life takes place when we are followers of Jesus. At Christmas time we enjoy the story of the babe in the manger, but he is not content to be kept in the manger. He comes into our lives to discard much that is not suitable for one of his followers: attitudes and behaviors which just don't fit a person who is preparing to live in the Father's house, the pride and arrogance which get in the way of following Jesus' example of service, and the anger and bitterness which sour many human relationships. They need to be replaced by love, joy, peace, patience, kindness, goodness, faithfulness, gentleness and self control. Then he rearranges the furniture of worship, recreation, work, play, family activities, prayer, study, and service so that each piece will fit into an appropriate design. Sometimes the process will involve much work and anguish, but the end result is much more pleasing.

Blessings as Jesus rearranges your furniture.

19

GLIMPSES OF GOD'S PRESENCE

Our Greatest Security

God is our refuge and strength, a very present help in trouble.

Psalm 46:1

London was a frightening place in 1939 as bombs were falling on the city nightly. Thousands of English children were evacuated into rural areas to remove them from danger and spare them from fear. But there was an unanticipated threat to the children in the remote areas. Removed from the love and security provided by their parents, they suffered emotional disturbances. The children felt greater security when they were with their parents, even though the bombs might be falling.

We may have grown far beyond the years when we were considered children, and yet our situation is similar to that of those children of England. Life provides us with multiple reasons for anxiety, apprehension, worry, fear, or concern. God has never promised that he will spare us from every adversity and trial in this life, but he has promised that he will never abandon us when the journey becomes hard and dangers threaten us on every side. Our greatest security is not in being removed from the bombardments of life, but in knowing that we are surrounded with the protecting care of a loving Father in the midst of life's dangers. The Psalmist lived with that confidence as he wrote, "The Lord is my light and my salvation; whom shall I fear? The Lord is the stronghold of my life; of whom shall I be afraid?" (Ps. 27:1). We can approach life with the same confidence because we know there is a risen Lord and Savior who promises to be with us today, and ultimately he will come and take us to himself.

Blessings as God takes your fears to himself by surrounding you with his loving arms today.

IN DAILY LIFE

Choices

Now if you are unwilling to serve the Lord, choose
this day whom you will serve...but as for me and
my household, we will serve the Lord.

Joshua 24:15

Playboy magazine wanted to include Ben Hamilton, a center on the University of Minnesota football team, in a group photo of its preseason All-America team in the October 2000 issue. He felt that appearing in the magazine would not be true to his Christian convictions saying, "It just came down to something I didn't want to be associated with. I've seen the magazine, and I know what it's about. It's not something I want to be a part of." Some people razzed him about it, but many appreciated his stand. He said, "I've gotten more support than I thought I would. People respect you for what you believe in."

I appreciate the congruity between Ben's belief and behavior. We probably won't be asked to appear in *Playboy*, but every day each of us is faced with choices which test the relationship between our belief and behavior. There are constant pressures to put belief in the back seat.

The promise is that God does not abandon us, but is with us to empower us to make behavior choices consistent with being followers of Jesus. Paul wrote to his Corinthian friends, "No testing has overtaken you that is not common to everyone. God is faithful, and he will not let you be tested beyond your strength, but with the testing he will also provide the way out so that you may be able to endure it" (I Cor. 10:13).

Blessings as you draw on the power of his presence with you today.

*God's Presence in
Living and Growing
as a Christian*

IN LIVING AND GROWING AS A CHRISTIAN

Not Very Good At First

I will sing to the Lord as long as I live; I will sing praise to my God while I have being.

Psalm 104:33

"I might not be very good at first," commented our granddaughter as she contemplated taking piano lessons. On one visit to our home, her mother started to show her something about how the notes on the page related to the keys on the piano, and she was diligently working on a one finger endeavor to play the first phrase of "Lead on O King Eternal." We were amazed at how rapidly she was learning, but she was right: she will not be very good at first. But you could hear in the way she expressed it that she was determined to play the piano well some day.

"I might not be very good at first." Is that how it goes with us in being followers of Jesus, as well? Do we look back on how we have played the melody of life and realize that there have been many notes out of harmony with the way our Lord has written the music?

I can certainly answer, "Yes." But I know that there is a teacher who has instructed, corrected, and encouraged me through the years. Through the guidance of the Holy Spirit there has been some changing of attitudes and behavior so that the hymn has become somewhat more harmonious. As we spend time under his tutelage, we will make progress in living out our faith, and be enabled to hit those notes of love, joy, peace, patience, kindness, goodness, gentleness, and self control with greater clarity and enthusiasm.

Blessings as the Spirit energizes and inspires you in the melody of life.

GLIMPSES OF GOD'S PRESENCE

Nurse Logs

*Let each of you look not to your own interest, but
to the interests of others.*

Philippians 2:4

Lofty firs, cedars and hemlocks towered over our heads and the sound of cascading water surrounded Marilyn and me as we walked through the Deception Falls Park in the Washington Cascade Mountains. Sunlight filtered through the trees to highlight the low growing plants. What a refreshing time in God's green cathedral!

On the ground we saw several nurse logs–trees which had helped beautify this place and enrich the earth's oxygen supply in the distant past. Having reached maturity and fallen years ago, their decaying remains were providing a place for seeds to sprout and new trees to begin their reach toward the sky. An interpretive sign by one of them stated that these trees could grow for 500 years, and then the fallen logs could provide nourishment encouraging new life for another 500 years.

I began to think, "I want to be like a nurse log, helping to make life good and beautiful around me while I live, and leaving a heritage which will be helpful for others beyond the days of my life." Being a nurse log–it can happen as we first sink our roots deep into God's grace through Jesus Christ. Drawing on the nourishment we receive from him through Word and Sacraments we can grow straight and tall, reaching toward the heavens, bringing beauty, grace and purity to those around us. Living under the guidance of the Holy Spirit we will leave a heritage which will be a blessing to those who come after us.

Blessings as you help bring life and new growth among God's people.

26

IN LIVING AND GROWING AS A CHRISTIAN

Enhanced Melodies

I can do all things through him who strengthens me.
Philippians 4:13

Dr. Alvin Rogness in his book *The Age and You* tells about a young girl in a tourist hotel in Norway playing a one finger melody each morning, annoying the other guests. One morning the great musician, Edvard Grieg, hearing the performance went to the piano, took the child in his lap, and enhanced the melody with beautiful harmonies which delighted the guests. Rogness likens this to the way the imperfect melodies of our lives can be transformed into the "music of heaven" when the Master gets involved.

Sometimes we attempt to play the melody of forgiveness. It is often hard for us as we try to deal with real hurts, but our feeble attempts sound richer when Jesus takes us in his lap, envelops us in his forgiveness and fills us with gratitude which helps us to be more forgiving.

As we try to play the melody of faith and commitment we find that doubts and self-interest produce sour notes. But Jesus comes to take us in his lap, reminding us that he is with us always, that there is nothing in all creation that can separate us from his love. When we are drawn close to him, the melody finds new harmonies.

There are those good and happy occasions of celebration when we play the melody of joy. Even that melody can be enriched when Christ is a part of life, and we experience the spirit which prompted Paul to write to his Philippian friends, "Rejoice in the Lord always; again I will say, Rejoice" (Phil. 4:4).

Blessings as your melodies are enhanced by Jesus.

GLIMPSES OF GOD'S PRESENCE

Tethered

The law was our disciplinarian until Christ came,
so that we might be justified by faith.

Galatians 3:24

When I was a very young child my parents tied me up with a rope. Was that child abuse? Definitely not. Dad had planted a field of corn near the house, and one day this little youngster wandered out into it. My parents realized that if the corn had been any higher they would not have seen their little boy. So, until after the corn was cut, I was tethered to the clothes line whenever I played outside. I wonder if I was frustrated by the restriction. Now I am glad that my parents cared enough about me to take steps to keep me from getting lost in the corn field.

God, motivated by his love for us, has given us commandments which are intended to be a tether which keeps us from danger. Many behaviors, attitudes and activities may lure us to wander in their direction, but in the end they make us lose sight of the Father. When someone wrongs us it seems right that we should get revenge, but God's Word tells us, "No. Love and forgive your enemy." When we desire power and control, the Word calls us to be servants of one another.

Who among us has not felt some frustration when God's commands restrain us from going into the "corn fields" which seem to be a delightful place to play. As we mature as followers of Jesus we begin to realize that the commands and admonitions come from a loving Father who wants to save us from disaster.

Blessings as you live in harmony with God's great purpose for you.

The Construction Crew

Since you are eager for spiritual gifts, strive to excel in them for building up the church.

I Corinthians 14:12

After the worship service one Sunday I saw a man standing alone. Wanting him to feel welcome at the church, I went over to strike up a conversation with him. It was not long before words of criticism were flowing from his mouth. Homosexuals, politicians, preachers, and teachers were targets of his venom. My thought: "How can I get away from this guy?"

Contrast some other people:

Gloria always has a word of encouragement for those she greets at church.

Jeff teaches teens the Bible and spends time with them outside Sunday School.

Mary and Joe invite church visitors to their home for a meal.

It seems that the people in the last group are part of a construction crew, while the first person I mentioned is a demolition crew. Those on the demolition crew complain, criticize, belittle, discourage. The construction folks encourage, build up, support, compliment, speak well of others. Which would you rather be around?

It is hard to build up if we have not been built up. In his ministry Jesus often reached out to the "throwaways" of his society to draw them into the company of his followers where they were

GLIMPSES OF GOD'S PRESENCE

made whole and able to be a part of his construction crew. Paul reminds us that if any one is in Christ Jesus, he is a new creation. In the presence of Jesus we are lifted up, moved to gratitude, and empowered to lift others up.

Blessings as you find joy in being on the construction crew.

IN LIVING AND GROWING AS A CHRISTIAN

A New Song

*Sing to the Lord a new song, his praise from the
end of the earth!*

Isaiah 42:10

The newspaper carried a story about a large group of humpback whales near Australia which is now singing an entirely new song brought in by a few outsiders. Apparently the song which humpbacks sing depends upon where they live. In the different ocean basins the whales have created their particular vocalizations which change only gradually over time. But the Australian whales quickly adopted a new pattern brought in by some whales which migrated from another area.

I see a parallel between the whales' songs and the patterns of our lives. Those patterns and mores are certainly shaped by the culture around us. Some of us who have been around for a while see it in the conformity of teen agers in terms of dress, vocabulary, and behavior. We may chuckle a bit as we think of our own teenage years. Even as we move beyond those years there is a tendency to "sing the same song" as our peers. We are definitely influenced by the culture around us.

The good news of Jesus has moved into our world calling us to sing a new song in our orientation, thoughts, and behavior–the song of heaven. That's why Paul writes to his friends in Rome, "Do not be conformed to this world, but be transformed by the renewing of your minds, so that you may discern what is the will of God–what is good and acceptable and perfect" (Rom. 12:2).

31

GLIMPSES OF GOD'S PRESENCE

We are living in an estranged sea, but we have heard the new song of God's mercy and grace through Jesus.

Blessings as you sing the new song today.

IN LIVING AND GROWING AS A CHRISTIAN

Building A Nest

*Everyone then who hears these words of mine and
acts on them will be like a wise man who built his
house on rock.*

Matthew 7:24

High atop the highest power pole in the middle of a Wenatchee, WA, railroad yard, two ospreys decided to build their nest. It was an excellent lookout, but far more dangerous than the birds realized because the branches they used to build their nest dangled dangerously near the power lines, raising the twin dangers of a power outage and a fire which could destroy the nest.

Early one morning linemen from the Chelan County Public Utility District began digging a hole 50 feet from the nesting pole. By mid day they had placed a 75 foot pole in the hole, and then two men in a cherry picker bucket were lifted up to the nest. Carefully they moved the nest onto the bucket, and then transferred it to a nest-sized platform atop the new pole where the ospreys could lay eggs and raise their young in safety.

The story prompted reflection on the risks we face in "building our nests" in dangerous places. Thoughtlessly, we can put our spiritual lives at risk as we construct our work nests, our social nests, our recreational nests, our attitudinal nests and our friendship nests. We are encouraged to build our nests in safe places by think-ing about matters which are true, honorable, just, pure, lovely,

GLIMPSES OF GOD'S PRESENCE

gracious, worthy of praise, and excellent (Phil. 4:8) and by setting our minds on things that are above (Col. 3:2). As we prayerfully hear and read God's Word, the Holy Spirit will guide us and enable us to fly to safe nesting sites.

Blessings as you construct your nests.

IN LIVING AND GROWING AS A CHRISTIAN

Qualified

*I pray that, according to the riches of his glory,
(God) may grant that you may be strengthened in
your inner being with power through his Spirit.*
Ephesians 3:16

A friend sent me a message which contained the sentence, "God doesn't call the qualified, he qualifies the called." Think of those twelve disciples Jesus chose. Can you imagine a newly elected president choosing such a bunch of "nobodies" for his cabinet? It does not appear that any of them held any important positions in their society. There was real potential for conflict as he chose Simon, the Zealot (passionately anti-Roman), and Matthew, the tax collector (a Roman collaborator). Certainly the twelve would have been considered unqualified for spearheading a new religious movement. Being with Jesus changed them–qualified them.

Paul saw that happening in the Christian church as he wrote, "Consider your own call...not many of you were wise by human standards, not many were powerful....But God chose what is foolish in the world to shame the wise; God chose what is weak in the world to shame the strong" (I Cor. 1:26-27).

Are you aware of situations where someone has responded, "Oh, I could never do that!" when asked to do something in the life of the church. How different the statement of Paul, "I can do all things through him who strengthens me" (Phil 4:13). Yes, there

GLIMPSES OF GOD'S PRESENCE

may be physical, mental, or emotional limitations in our lives, yet many of us have discovered that God does work in and through us in ways we may not have dreamed possible. Being with Jesus makes a difference today just as it did for the twelve.

Blessings as God calls and qualifies you.

IN LIVING AND GROWING AS A CHRISTIAN

In the Shelter of God's Love

*For you have been a refuge to the poor, a refuge
to the needy in their distress, a shelter from the
rainstorm and a shade from the heat.*

Isaiah 25:4

We are privileged to view a beautiful, thriving lavender rhododendron plant from our front window. Many rhododendrons do not fare as well in this area because of climate conditions. In fact, the landscaper planted another one at the same time about 40 feet away in the neighboring yard. It did not survive the first year, and has been removed.

What has made the difference for those two plants? I believe it is because ours was planted in a more sheltered location. Behind it is the wall on the northwest side of the garage, and it is nestled between two large rocks, each of which is about 18 inches high and two feet wide. There it is protected from the heat of the summer sun and the cold of the winter winds. The plant in our neighbor's yard was in a position to be exposed to both sun and cold wind.

As human beings we are confronted by adversities, temptations, trials, and tragedies which can be just as devastating to us as hot sun and cold winds are to rhododendrons. Some people don't do very well in struggling with hardships, while others seem to come through beautifully. There may be a wide variety of factors involved in how we pull through, but many followers of Jesus have learned that they can trust the promise of being sheltered through life's storms by the loving presence of God. Blessings as you thrive in the shelter of God's love.

GLIMPSES OF GOD'S PRESENCE

Reflecting the Light

Wash me, and I shall be whiter than snow.
Psalm 51:7

I was feeling sorry for my Arizona and California friends one winter morning as I was removing about two inches of snow from my driveway. The morning temperature was about twenty degrees with no suggestion of a breeze, and there wasn't a cloud in the sky. The brilliant sun sparkled off the snow so that it appeared that someone had scattered a truckload of diamonds. Marilyn and I commented several times about what a gorgeous sight it was.

It's amazing how much the fresh snow magnifies the intensity of the sun's rays, and everything seems so much brighter. There seems to be an analogy here with the Christian life. Is there not a sense in which Christians can reflect the light of Jesus, who is the Light of the world, to bring brightness into every day life? As Christ dwells in us we will reflect more of his love and compassion in a world which has been dirtied by our living out of harmony with God.

Too often I have been like the snow which has been on the ground for a while and has started to get dirty so that it absorbs rather than reflects brightness. But the promise is that we can brighten this world. Jesus tells his disciples. "Let your light shine before others, so that they may see your good works and give glory to your Father in heaven" (Matt. 5:16).

38

IN LIVING AND GROWING AS A CHRISTIAN

As you are aware of the darkness in the world today, aren't you thankful that God has called you to bring some brightness into it, and has promised to be with you to help you do it?

Blessings as you reflect the Light today.

GLIMPSES OF GOD'S PRESENCE

The Spinning Wheel

The free gift of God is eternal life in Christ Jesus our Lord.

Romans 6:23

A well-preserved spinning wheel has a prominent place in our living room. It came from Norway sometime before 1860. Some grooves in the spindle indicate that it has been well used.

One summer eight-year-old Marilyn was visiting the farm in Minnesota where her mother grew up. Her uncle took her to an upstairs storage room, showed her the spinning wheel, and asked, "Would you like to have it?" She quickly responded, "Yes." So he shipped it home with her.

Recently Marilyn looked at the spinning wheel and commented that she did not realize what a treasure she was receiving at the time. Now it stands as a reminder of a family heritage, stretching through American pioneers and back into an unknown origin in Norway. A heritage of hard work, caring hearts, and Christian faith is embodied in those who have spent time at the wheel.

We talked about a parallel experience in our Christian faith. At the time our parents brought us to the font for baptism we had no conception of what it meant. As children, growing up in Christian homes, we began to understand more of God's love for us. As we have reached senior years, we have a much deeper appreciation for the wondrous gift God has given us in Jesus, and for the

IN LIVING AND GROWING AS A CHRISTIAN

heritage of faith which has been passed on by faithful followers of Jesus. Yet we realize that as long as we are confined to these bodies we see reality only dimly, but we look forward to when we will understand even more fully the wonder of God's gracious love.

Blessings as you grow in appreciation of God's great gift.

Call Home

We do not know how to pray as we ought, but that very Spirit intercedes.

Romans 8:26

Bill was a beloved nursing home resident, suffering from the earlier stages of dementia. One day he was persistent in wanting to call his wife, so a staff member assisted him in dialing the phone number. When she answered he said, "Well, what did you want?"

While my mental faculties seem to be working at least well enough to keep me writing at this point in life, I sometimes feel somewhat similar to Bill as I live in a world where much seems to be confusing and disorienting. I don't comprehend the values which seem to motivate the behavior of many. I can understand the desire for more wealth, but why is accumlation rated so highly when many in this world are living in abject poverty? I can understand the longing for power and control, but why exercise them to the detriment of other peoples' well being? And yet, living in a culture which puts taking care of self at the pinnacle of the priority list encourages me to do the same.

It's time to make a phone call home asking, "Well, Lord, what do you want? What do you want me to do? How do you want me to live in this world? How do you want me to manage the gifts you have entrusted to me?" It becomes a two-way conversation as I ask the questions in prayer and then listen to his reply through the Holy Scriptures which point me to Jesus who is his Word to me. As I listen I hear a voice of love and compassion guiding me through the confusion of the world.

Blessings as you phone home.

IN LIVING AND GROWING AS A CHRISTIAN

After the Fire

We also boast in our sufferings, knowing that suffering produces endurance, and endurance produces character, and character produces hope.
Romans 5:3, 4

The Longleaf Pine needs to go through fire before it can grow to become a tree. A new seedling grows in the form of grass, develops a strong root system with long needles shielding the stem bud underground, and waits for fire. When it has been burned it starts growing upward, becoming a tall tree. At one time there were millions of acres of the pines in the coastal plains of the Southeast, but now they cover only about two percent of their original area. One of the main reasons for the decline is the human effort to prevent forest fires.

As the absence of fire is a detriment to the pine forests, so affluence and ease can be a hindrance to the Christian Church. As fire stimulates the growth of the pines, so adversity and trial can stimulate the growth of Christian faith. As I hear stories about the Church around the world it seems that the Church is more alive in those parts of the world where life is hard and people do not have much of this world's goods.

Perhaps you have known Christians whose faith has been strengthened through adversity when they have experienced being upheld by the presence of God in a way they never knew in their times of ease. Probably none of us will pray, "Lord, give me suffering," but we can live in the assurance that if it comes our way, God is with us to turn the adversity into an opportunity for growth.

Blessings as you cherish the presence of God in your difficult days.

GLIMPSES OF GOD'S PRESENCE

Choosing Your Face

Wisdom makes one's face shine, and the hardness
of one's countenance is changed.

Ecclesiastes 8:1

I think it was supposed to be a fancy hairdo, but to me the hair looked about as wild as mine when I get out of bed in the morning...and that is pretty bad. The set of her mouth was surly, and antagonism radiated from her eyes. Her expression said, "Don't cross me," or "I'm going to get you." I think there was the potential for beauty in that face, but toughness had cancelled out the beauty. Marilyn and I were both repelled by that image on the cover of the magazine, and we made sure we laid it face down.

We wondered why the editors of the magazine chose that picture when there is so much beauty which could be portrayed. We pondered why that person, and so many like her, want to project the kind of image which says, "I am tough and ugly inside," rather than the image of kindness and goodness. And then I questioned, "Have there been times when I have let the ugliness within me be reflected toward others?"

There is much in this world which encourages us to show our worst face, but as followers of Jesus we have been promised the presence of the Holy Spirit in our lives to overcome that temptation. We are reminded that the fruits of the Spirit are love, joy, peace, patience, kindness, goodness, faithfulness, gentleness, and self-control (Galatians 5:22, 23). As we allow those fruits to grow within us, our faces and our lives will bring a blessing to all who come into contact with us.

Blessings as you grow in beauty and grace.

IN LIVING AND GROWING AS A CHRISTIAN

A Bird of Many Songs

O sing to the Lord a new song, for he has done marvelous things .... Make a joyful noise to the Lord, all the earth; break forth into joyous song and sing praises.

Psalm 98:1, 4

Which song bird has a whole songbook to choose from? While most birds have only one song, most mockingbirds can master at least 180 in a few months. They have a marvelous ability to imitate the songs of other birds, as well as the sounds of squirrels, frogs, crickets, sirens, and a rusty gate. One story is told of a mockingbird which mimicked an alarm clock so perfectly that it awakened residents early every morning. But the mockingbird has no song of its own.

We, like the mockingbird, hear all kinds of "songs" around us. Some are filled with the strident sounds of anger and aggressiveness. Some carry the pleasing notes of kindness and thoughtfulness. Others are filled with the harshness of cursing and vileness. Demeaning notes fill some. Sometimes we hear the joyful rhapsody of thanksgiving. And the list goes on.

Also, like the mockingbird, we have a great capacity for imitating what we hear. Which of the many songs we hear do we choose to sing? I'm convinced we have much reason to sing the beautiful melodies of praise and thanksgiving. God has created us in a very marvelous way which calls for a song of thanksgiving. He has

GLIMPSES OF GOD'S PRESENCE

shown his love for us most powerfully in Jesus, which inspires a song of praise in many a heart. Many of us have known his presence to uphold, encourage, guide, and bless us. We find a song of joy to be a proper response.

Blessings as you choose your songs today.

IN LIVING AND GROWING AS A CHRISTIAN

Antidote To Worry

Do not worry, saying, "What will we eat?" or "What will we drink?" or "What will we wear?"...your heavenly Father knows that you need all these things.

Matthew 6:31-32

A newspaper story quoted a cancer patient saying, "Worry is like sitting in a rocking chair. It gives you something to do, but doesn't get you anywhere."

I like that attitude. All of us wish we could be freed from our worries, fretting, and anxiety. We wish we could get out of that rocking chair, and get on to more productive things. It is not always that easy. It seems that some people have a natural propensity to worry more than others. How can we deal with it?

The Apostle Paul points us in the right direction as he writes, "Do not worry about anything, but in everything by prayer and supplication with thanksgiving let your requests be made known to God. And the peace of God, which surpasses all understanding, will guard your hearts and your minds in Christ Jesus" (Phil. 4:6, 7). Notice that he mentions prayer with thanksgiving. I'm convinced that if our prayers center only on our own problems, we will keep sitting in the rocking chair. But if we set our minds on thanking and praising God, we open our hearts to that peace of God which enables us to get out of the chair and move forward with our lives.

Blessings as you remember God's promises and his presence, and are moved to thanksgiving and praise.

GLIMPSES OF GOD'S PRESENCE

The Corrections

Correct me, O Lord, but in just measure; not in your anger.

Jeremiah 10:24

After writing an e-mail devotional I usually give it to Marilyn to read before sending it. Each time I hope that she will tell me that she likes it. That happens quite often. But there are other times when she is very direct in offering some suggestions for change. I am not nearly as happy about those times. After some initial resistance I usually recognize that her suggestions need to be incorporated into the writing. The end result is a better devotional, and I am thankful for the input of a loving spouse.

Something parallel happens in our faith journey as the Holy Spirit speaks to us through the Scriptures, sermons, other followers of Jesus, and our own consciences. There are times when we are happy that we have expressed kindness, shown some patience, or given some evidence of other fruits of the Spirit. But there are other times when we do not like being reminded of how often we fall short of what God has intended for our lives, and are not excited about the work required to change life patterns which are obstacles to our spiritual growth.

As we take time to reflect, we recognize that it is a loving God who seeks to guide us toward wholeness, goodness, integrity, and what is best for our lives. When we make the effort to pay attention to him, we will end up thanking him for his concern and his guidance. Hopefully, all of us can look back and say, "Yes, my life has been made better because of the Spirit's direction."

Blessings as you receive the Spirit's correction and direction.

IN LIVING AND GROWING AS A CHRISTIAN

Square, Plumb and Level

All scripture is inspired by God and is useful for teaching, for reproof, for correction, and for training in righteousness.

II Timothy 3:16

"There are three important principles in building: square, plumb and level. None of them exist," a construction worker grumbled as he was handling rain gutters which didn't fit because the principles had not been applied to the sections of the roof on which they were to be installed. Anyone who has done some house remodeling has experienced the frustration of encountering building parts which are not square, plumb or level.

Followers of Jesus are called to measure up to some primary standards as we build our lives, including love for God and other people, loyalty to Christ, steadfast faith, integrity, kindness, humility, patience, generosity, etc. Some self-examination convinces us that we have something in common with those framers who did not get every corner square, every window level, or every wall plumb. Thankfully, God, who desires excellence as we frame our lives, does not remove us from his crew if we fail to reach perfection, but offers us his forgiveness through Jesus.

If we manage to come somewhat close to getting it right, it is because the Holy Spirit is working in us. He uses the Word of God to help us build our lives according to his master plan. So, while God is not finished with us yet, we can be grateful that he has been at work in the building of our lives. His presence gives us joy in that construction project.

Blessings as you build your life under the guidance of God's Spirit.

GLIMPSES OF GOD'S PRESENCE

The Power of Words

The word of God is living and active, sharper than any two-edged sword...it is able to judge the thoughts and intentions of the heart.

Hebrews 4:12

Sir George Adam Smith has told a story about being in a group journeying through the Arabian desert. They were met by some Muslims who gave his party the customary greeting, "Peace be upon you." When they learned that he, a Christian, was in the group, they returned to ask back the greeting, for a Muslim greeting had been extended to one they considered an infidel.

The story illustrates the understanding of the power of words prevalent in the Middle East. In contrast, our culture looks upon talk as cheap, and we say, "Sticks and stones may break my bones, but words can never hurt me."

In reality, many of us have experienced the power of words. We have seen their power to hurt, discourage and tear down. We have also known the power to heal, build up and encourage.

There is power in the Word of God. The creation story in Genesis 1 affirms that power in the repeated phrase, "And God said, 'Let there be...,' and there was ...."

There is power in the recreative Word of God:

That word of his love and grace in Jesus;

50

IN LIVING AND GROWING AS A CHRISTIAN

That word that you are accepted and forgiven through the life and death of Jesus;

That word which makes new people out of those who trust him;

That word which shapes and forms your words, making them words which build up rather than tear down.

Blessings as you are shaped by that Word, and as you let it shape your words.

GLIMPSES OF GOD'S PRESENCE

God and Success

If any want to become my followers, let them deny
themselves and take up their cross and follow me.
Matthew 16:24

"God and success go together," the huge billboard blatantly pro-claimed. Apparently the sponsoring church wanted us to believe that if we come to that church we will find a relationship with God which will make us successful. I wonder how that message would sound to Jesus as he hung on the cross. What would Paul's reaction be as he served time in prison, or when he was being stoned? How would it play to our faithful brothers and sisters in Christ in Africa, many of whom have a vibrant faith, but little of this world's goods?

Jesus did not promise us success, but he did promise something much more important–life. "I came that they may have life, and have it abundantly" (John 10:10). He gives us a new quality of life as the Spirit of God dwells in us and we experience the peace and joy flowing from a solid relationship with God. It is life which knows that we are embraced in the love of God whether we are rich or poor. It is the life of faith which I have been privileged to witness in many followers of Jesus through their days of trial. It is life in which we are called to carry the cross with Jesus in the grand enterprise of the Kingdom of God. It is life with a new con-cern which knows the satisfaction of reaching out to be a blessing through serving others. Many have demonstrated to me that the new life which Jesus gives is much more important than success.

Blessings as you rejoice in the gift of abundant life today.

IN LIVING AND GROWING AS A CHRISTIAN

Carrying the Cross

*I am now rejoicing in my sufferings for your sake,
and in my flesh I am completing what is lacking in
Christ's afflictions for the sake of his body, that is,
the church.*

Colossians 1:24

About six months after her husband's death, her doctor informed her that she must have a risky surgery. A few weeks earlier she had learned that her daughter had cancer. She sighed, "I have a very heavy cross to bear." A friend commented (not to her), "That's not a cross. Those are common events of life."

Which of the two was correct? The burdened woman was using an expression which she had heard many times in describing such trials, so according to common usage she was bearing a cross. But the friend was also right, because she knew the origins of the expression went back to Jesus who was talking about the cross which comes specifically because we are followers of Jesus. As followers, we may be called upon to make sacrifices for the sake of the Kingdom of God. What the cross means will differ from person to person. While carrying the cross may be difficult, followers of Jesus have known that it is a privilege to be engaged in the grand enterprise of the Kingdom of God by joining with Jesus in carrying the cross for the sake of others.

When we are fearful and hesitant about taking up the cross, we are reminded that our Lord does not abandon us to make us carry

53

GLIMPSES OF GOD'S PRESENCE

it alone. In fact, the times we are struggling under the cross assigned to us are likely to be the times we experience the closest fellowship with our Lord.

Blessings as you carry the cross fashioned for you by God's grace.

IN LIVING AND GROWING AS A CHRISTIAN

No Room For a Wet Blanket

I will give thanks to the Lord with my whole heart....
I will be glad and exult in you.

Psalm 91-2

I should have known better that day in the bank, but I asked, "How are you?" "I don't like what the Federal Reserve is doing in lowering the interest rates. I can't afford that," she replied.

Marilyn had met the same woman a few days earlier, and there was something else to complain about that day. She is a good woman in many ways, but we are finding that we have to resist the temptation to avoid her because of her complaining.

Our experience with her causes me to examine my own behavior. Do I sometimes spoil someone's day through complaining? Or do I bring joy and peace to others through a positive, thankful spirit? There are statements in the Scriptures that we should encourage one another, and build one another up. I don't recall any admonitions to be a wet blanket on someone's day. (Exception: if we are opposing injustice, some people will not be happy with us.)

While there are many reasons to complain, there is more reason for joy and thanksgiving. The way to a joyful spirit is to pay more attention to God's goodness toward us than to the problems, hurts and inconveniences of life. He has placed us in a wonderfully created world where we are surrounded by beauty and the fascinating workings of his creation. Even more remarkable is his

GLIMPSES OF GOD'S PRESENCE

incomprehensible grace which moved him to come to us in Jesus to draw us into his embrace. How can we be mired down in complaining when surrounded by such beauty, love and grace?

Blessings as the love of God inspires you today.

IN LIVING AND GROWING AS A CHRISTIAN

Green Grass

May the God of peace...make you complete in everything good so that you may do his will, working among us that which is pleasing in his sight.

Hebrews 13:20, 21

Have you dyed any grass green recently? That happened in our back yard and throughout the Planned Unit Development in which we once lived. While spraying our lawn for weeds, an in-experienced machine operator applied too much spray in many places, leaving brown grass as well as dead weeds. We were told that it would take several weeks for the grass to come back. In the meantime the brown grass was dyed green. The dyed dead grass was very distinguishable from living grass, but from a distance the mistakes were not quite so obvious. The problem was not really solved until new grass grew up from the roots.

Not many of us have ever dyed grass, but have we attempted to disguise ethical mistakes, moral lapses, and sin in our lives? Sometimes we can do a pretty good job of it. Sometimes, in fact, we hide our sins so well from others that we hide them from ourselves. Most often our cover-up is not that successful, and even if it is, there is One who can spot the dead grass in our lives.

What we need is not better cover-up methods, but healthy growth from good roots in good soil so that there will be less need for

57

GLIMPSES OF GOD'S PRESENCE

cover-ups. The good news of the Christian faith is that God is on the side of growth. When we abandon the cover-up mentality and let the Holy Spirit work within us we can begin to realize the joy of seeing new growth.

Blessings as you experience the excitement of spiritual growth.

Rage

Whoever wants to be first must be last of all and servant of all.

Mark 9:35

RAGE! We seldom heard the word just a few years ago, but now we frequently hear about another incident of rage: road rage, air rage, school rage, work place rage, athletic event rage, and the list goes on.

Some of the culprits blamed for rage are the increasingly rapid pace of life, the increased expectations to produce and to perform, violent programing on TV, overburdened transportation systems, etc. But if such external factors are the cause, why is it that some people don't seem to be overcome by anger even though they face the same circumstances as those who react with fury? There are, for instance, drivers who have made a decision to not react with rage, but when someone cuts in on them they will just drop back and give the aggressive driver plenty of space. I believe the real problem lies within us rather than outside us.

Jesus points us in a different direction as he has said, "I give you a new commandment, that you love one another" (John 13:34). Thankfully, Jesus does not just give us commands which we find it impossible to obey, but he lives in his people to transform us so that we might grow into his model of love and servanthood.

The most effective way to deal with impulses to anger is to pray

GLIMPSES OF GOD'S PRESENCE

that our hearts may be open to the gentle, transforming, recreative work of the Spirit in our lives. Many followers of Jesus have discovered the power of that prayer.

Blessings as the peace of God fills your life today.

IN LIVING AND GROWING AS A CHRISTIAN

Just a Little Thing

Do you not know that a little yeast leavens the whole batch of dough? Clean out the old yeast so that you may be a new batch.

I Corinthians 5:6, 7

The hundreth launch of the space shuttle program was postponed on October 10, 2000 because someone saw an eight ounce metal pin on an oxygen line between the shuttle and its huge, external fuel tank. The seven astronauts were already strapped into their seats when an inspection team noticed the pin. There was concern that the pin could ricochet between the shuttle and the fuel tank, possibly causing an explosion. Such serious consequences from so small an object!

The astronauts were probably disappointed that their flight was postponed, but I am sure that they were also very grateful for the sharp eyes which noticed the pin and saved them from possible disaster.

Sometimes there can be serious adverse consequences to our life of faith (as well as to other people) from attitudes, thoughts, words, or actions which may seem rather insignificant. Therefore, Paul's words to his friends in Corinth are ones which we could well heed: "Examine yourselves to see whether you are living in the faith" (II Cor. 13:5).

Christian self-examination is not meant to lead to miserable feelings of depression and an "I'm no good" mentality. Its result should be repentance, confession, the joy of forgiveness, and the

GLIMPSES OF GOD'S PRESENCE

removal of the dangerous "little things" from our lives. Yes, serious self-examination may lead to some disappointment, but the ultimate result is successful Christian living. Looking back, we will be thankful for the guidance of the Holy Spirit in looking for the dangerous little things.

Blessings as you pay attention to the little things.

IN LIVING AND GROWING AS A CHRISTIAN

Problem Trees

Bear fruits worthy of repentance.
Luke 3:8

The rural village of Zernikow, Germany had an embarrassing situation. In 1938 someone planted some larch trees amidst the pines outside the village. In the fall when the leaves turned a golden brown, a very prominent swastika could be seen from the air.

It would not take a very hard look at history to find many examples of human actions which have brought embarrassment, anguish, grief, inconvenience, and suffering to others long after the original actions. Perhaps a serious and impartial examination of our own lives would reveal some tell-tale larch trees. I see this story as a call to us to live our lives today so that they will not have adverse long term consequences for others.

If we see offensive trees in our own lives, we may still have the opportunity to cut some of them down. There may be some we will never be able to remove. Whatever trees we find, we can still hold on to the promise of God's Word that there is nothing in all creation that can separate us from God's love in Jesus Christ (Romans 8:39). We are forgiven through Jesus.

But there is more. We can move beyond past actions and their consequences. There is the promise that the Holy Spirit is with us

GLIMPSES OF GOD'S PRESENCE

and in us today to help us to avoid planting problem trees. His fruits in our lives are love, joy, peace, patience, kindness, goodness, faithfulness, humility, and self control (Galatians 5:22). When those qualities are a part of our lives, those who come after us will give thanks for the trees we have planted.

Blessings as you plant your trees today.

IN LIVING AND GROWING AS A CHRISTIAN

Reflecting God's Grace

Let your light shine before others, so that they may see your good works and give glory to your Father in heaven.

Matthew 5:16

There is a small curio cabinet located in a place in our house which never receives any direct sunlight. One day Marilyn noticed that some reflected sunlight was shining on it, indicating that the glass needed some cleaning. With the help of that reflected light she was able to see just where the smudges were and the glass became sparkling clean.

Then she turned to trace the pattern of sunlight which was coming through the living room window (also due for some cleaning) and reflecting off the cloudy fireplace glass. As she observed the reflected light she pondered how God can use less than perfect persons to transmit his grace and mercy so that lives can become more like God intends them to be.

All of us can think of how God's grace has come to us through less than perfect people, and we know that if we have been receptive to that grace we are better people because of it. We are grateful to those reflectors and transmitters of grace for what they have meant in shaping our lives.

We can also be encouraged to know that God can use us to bring his love and grace to others in spite of our failings and shortcomings. Yes, we continue to pray that his Spirit may work on us to

GLIMPSES OF GOD'S PRESENCE

clean us up so that the light of his grace is not diminished by lives that are out of harmony with God's love, but we are thankful that we can be transmitters of grace before we ever reach perfection.

Blessings as you transmit the light of God's grace to others.

IN LIVING AND GROWING AS A CHRISTIAN

The Impact of Choices

...but as for me and my household, we will serve the Lord.

Joshua 24:15

A friend told Marilyn and me about an anticipated move to a new city, which would entail locating a house, enrolling children in school, finding a new church, and changing many familiar life patterns. She spoke about wanting to find a good school district for the children, locating a church where the family could be actively involved, and then finding a house near the church to facilitate their participation. She understood there was a connection between her faith and locating a home.

Her thought process can serve as an example for all of us in applying our faith to the very practical aspects of daily life. Do we put ourselves in those places which make it easier to live out our relationship with Jesus, or do we often find ourselves in places which erect roadblocks for that relationship? That question may have implications not only geographically, but also socially, educationally, in our employment, as well as other areas of our lives. Common daily choices frequently play a part in determining whether the living out of our loyalty to Jesus is facilitated or hindered.

Blessings in your choices.

GLIMPSES OF GOD'S PRESENCE

Observation and Imitation

Therefore be imitators of God, as beloved children, and live in love, as Christ loved us and gave himself up for us.

Ephesians 5:1, 2

A nice looking, round, metal trash container stood at the end of a kitchen cabinet in our daughter's house. It had a lid which was opened by stepping on a pedal at the bottom of the can–a convenient and quick arrangement for scraping leftover scraps of food and putting other kitchen waste into the container. The lid fell securely into place when the foot was removed from the pedal.

After it had been used for several months the family began noticing some discarded items lying in varying places on the kitchen floor. It was a puzzling development until one day our daughter observed Charlie, the family beagle, move toward the container, stand on his rear legs, put his front paws high on the container, and then place a rear foot on the pedal to open the lid. Careful observance and imitation of his masters had paid off for Charlie.

Charlie can be an example for us in learning from and imitating our Master. The Christian Church confesses that Jesus is our Savior–but also our Lord. As we follow him we grow in our understanding of how life is lived in the Kingdom of God, and are encouraged and guided in that way of living. The reward is not some scraps of food which have been discarded, but receiving the Bread of Life and the Living Water which nourishes us for eternal life.

Blessings as you learn from and imitate your Master.

*God's Presence In
Prayer*

IN PRAYER

Seasoned Prayer

Devote yourselves to prayer; keeping alert in it with thanksgiving.

Colossians 4:2

During the sermon the pastor referred to I Thessalonians 5:17: "Pray without ceasing." The young confirmation student handed in her sermon notes with the quotation reading, "Pray without seasoning." I have thought of those sermon notes many times through the years and wondered how often God has found my prayers lacking in seasoning. They are often pretty repetitious, and in their routineness the spice of passion has been left out. Thankfully, he hasn't said our prayers must meet certain quality standards before he will pay any attention to them.

And yet, I'm sure God would not mind some seasoning in our prayers. We can see examples in the Psalms, running all the way from exuberant expressions of praise to the salty tears of laments. Certainly there is a place in our intercessions for the seasoning of deeply felt compassion. How about a good measure of joyful thanksgiving? You can undoubtedly think of other special spices you can add to your prayers.

Our prayers certainly need to be seasoned with words and actions in our daily lives which bring joy to God. One of the notes sounded in the Old Testament is that God hates religious ceremonies, sacrifices, and prayers when they are accompanied by lives of dishonesty, lying and oppressing the poor. Integrity, generosity, and love and concern for others add a good flavor to our prayers.

Blessings as you season those prayers.

71

GLIMPSES OF GOD'S PRESENCE

What's In a Name

I will do whatever you ask in my name.
John 14:13

I once wrote a check for one million dollars. It was properly filled out, dated, signed and bore my account number. But I am sure that if it had been written to you, you would not have wasted your time going to the bank to cash it. It was worth nothing. However, if you received such a check bearing Bill Gates's signature and written on his account, you would probably be very eager to take it to the bank.

As followers of Jesus we are invited to draw on an account bearing the name of Jesus–"Ask in my Name." His followers have experienced the power of that name in many astounding ways. But what does it mean to ask in Jesus' name? I am convinced it is more than just tacking his name at the end of our prayers. Think of those checks which have Bill Gates's signature. He would not sign them if they were not for a purpose that was in harmony with what he wanted. Similarly prayers in Jesus' name are those which flow out of a relationship with Jesus in which we have listened to him and been led by his Spirit. They are formed in harmony with Jesus' will for us and for this world.

Our Lord urges us to come to him in prayer. He is probably more eager for us to pray than we are to pray. As we learn to practice the art of prayer formed in response to listening to his Word, learning from him, and being guided by his Spirit, we will discover more and more the truth of his promise.

Blessings as you pray in Jesus' name.

IN PRAYER

Finding Room in the Closet

*Likewise the Spirit helps us in our weakness; for we
do not know how to pray as we ought, but that very
Spirit intercedes with sighs too deep for words.*
Romans 8:26

During a sermon our pastor quoted Jesus as saying, "When you pray, go into your closet and shut the door and pray to your Father who is in secret...." A mental image formed of me trying to get into my closet, and not being able to because there is too much stuff there. Maybe that's why I do such a poor job of praying–I have too much stuff in my closet. Possessions and things yes, but much more: a busy life, challenges, activities, obligations, interests, attitudes and concerns which claim my attention and inhibit prayer.

Oh, how hard it is for some of us to clean out that closet. Will power doesn't seem sufficient for the task. Perhaps one of our first prayers should be for the Holy Spirit to clean out the closet for us and to teach us to pray. Our Lord calls us to pray, and gives us his own example of how life becomes richer as it is framed in prayer.

Blessings in your prayer life.

GLIMPSES OF GOD'S PRESENCE

Our Father

When we cry, "Abba! Father!" it is that very Spirit bearing witness with our spirit that we are children of God, and if children, then heirs, heirs of God and joint heirs with Christ.

Romans 8:15-17

We pray, "Our Father who art in heaven."

Luther reminds us that God encourages us to believe we are his children and he is really our Father so that we can pray to him in complete confidence, just as children speak to their loving father.

What good news that is for those of us who have known loving fathers to whom we could bring our concerns at any time. And for those whose earthly fathers have been less than loving, it is good news to know that there is a Father who loves us, cares about us, and who listens to us when we come to him. I believe the Scriptures portray a God who is more willing to listen to us than we are to speak to him.

When I lived in Ritzville, WA and attended the high school basketball games there, it was interesting to observe various fathers. There were some who regularly yelled words of criticism when their sons made mistakes in their play. Others called out words of encouragement to their sons throughout the game. Jesus shows us a God who fits the latter image.

Jesus teaches us to pray, "Our Father" rather than "My Father," reminding us that we are linked together with others of his followers whenever we pray.

Blessings as you find joy, comfort and hope in praying to our Father.

74

IN PRAYER

Hallowed Be Thy Name

Holy, holy, holy is the Lord of hosts; the whole earth is full of his glory.

Isaiah 6:3

We pray, "Hallowed be thy name."

In the Catechism Luther reminds us that God's name is holy in itself, but in this petition we ask that we may keep it holy, and this happens as his Word is taught in its truth and purity and when we live in harmony with it.

Hallowing God's name is thus much more than avoiding certain words. We see and hear much dishonoring of God's name all around us every day. Words of anger and criticism, and actions which have an adverse impact on others dishonor God and bring discord into his good world.

We, as children of God, have the opportunity to bring a different spirit into this world, reflective of his Spirit who lives in us. We can be a blessing to this world as we hallow God's name by speaking words which bring joy to our Heavenly Father, and behaving in a manner which reflects his good purpose for this world. What a privilege, and what a joy!!

Blessings on you as you keep his Name holy today.

GLIMPSES OF GOD'S PRESENCE

Thy Kingdom Come

The kingdom of God is not coming with things that can be observed; nor will they say, "Look, here it is!" or "There it is!" For, in fact, the kingdom of God is among you.

Luke 17:20, 21

We pray, "Thy kingdom come."

Luther reminds us that God's kingdom comes even if we don't pray for it, but in this petition we ask that it may come to us. This happens when our heavenly Father gives us his Holy Spirit, so that we trust his Word and live a God-fearing life both now and in eternity.

The major theme of Jesus' preaching and teaching is that the kingdom of God is at hand. He starts several of his parables by saying, "The kingdom of God is like...." As we listen to him we sense that the kingdom is not a geographical territory, but rather God's kingly rule taking place in people. That is the thought Luther picks up as he says the kingdom comes to us as we believe his Word and live a godly life.

God's kingdom is a gift of his grace to you and me for this day. We rejoice in the gift of his Spirit who draws us to faith, and makes it possible for us to be included in God's kingly rule of grace. He is with us today helping us to live that godly life, and to know the joy of it.

Blessings as you live in his kingdom.

IN PRAYER

Thy Will Be Done

*Be transformed by the renewing of your minds, so
that you may discern what is the will of God.*
Romans 12:2

We pray, "Thy will be done on earth as it is in heaven."

In the Small Catechism Luther reminds us that God's will is done even if we don't pray for it, but here we ask that it may be done also among us. This happens when God thwarts the devil's evil schemes, the world's corrupting influences, and our self-centeredness, which prevent us from keeping his name holy and oppose the coming of his kingdom. His will is also done as he strengthens our faith and keeps us firm in his Word.

Dream of what this world would be like if everyone did God's will. Newspapers and news programs would have no wars, crime, or violence to report. Envy, slander, greed and power struggles would give way to a world enjoying the harmony God intended for his creation. Self-destructive behavior would be unknown.

We may become discouraged about praying this petition because it doesn't seem that God intervenes in all the wrong in this world to impose his will. Yet people of faith keep on praying. We dare to believe that the petition counts for something and that God is working in his mysterious ways to keep this world from total evil and chaos. As we pray he sends his Spirit to help us do his will in our personal lives, motivating and enabling us to contribute to making this world a little better place.

Blessings as God helps you do his will.

77

GLIMPSES OF GOD'S PRESENCE

Our Daily Bread

God is able to provide you with every blessing in abundance, so that by having enough of everything, you may share abundantly....He who supplies seed to the sower and bread for food will supply and multiply your seed for sowing and increase the harvest of your righteousness.

II Corinthians 9:8,10

We pray, "Give us this day our daily bread."

Luther reminds us that even if we don't pray, God gives daily bread to all people, but we ask in this petition that he will help us to realize this and to receive our daily bread with gratitude. Then he defines daily bread as including everything needed for this life, and he lists such things as food, clothing, home, property, work, income, a devoted family, an orderly community, good government, favorable weather, peace, health, a good name, and true friends and neighbors. That pretty much covers it.

There are people in this world who live a hand-to-mouth existence where the issue of bread for today is very pertinent. Others of us have been able to accumulate enough of this world's resources so that we don't feel the pressure to ask God for bread for this day. Sometimes natural disasters rouse us out of our complacency to realize that we are truly dependent upon God's provision to sustain each heartbeat and each breath of air.

IN PRAYER

Marilyn says that when she prays this part of the Lord's Prayer she always thinks, "Thank you, Lord." We are indeed blessed, and so are those around us if we can live with a thankful spirit.

Blessings as you receive God's bountiful provision with gratitude.

Forgive Us

Bear with one another and, if anyone has a complaint against another, forgive each other; just as the Lord has forgiven you, so you also must forgive.

Colossians 3:13

We pray, "Forgive us our trespasses as we forgive those who trespass against us."

Again I turn to Luther for comment on this petition. In the Small Catechism he tells us that in this prayer we ask our heavenly Father not to hold our sins against us and, because of them, refuse to hear our prayers. We rely on his grace for forgiveness, admitting that we sin every day and deserve nothing but punishment. Responding to his grace we will forgive those who sin against us.

While the ability to forgive seems to come more naturally for some people than others, probably all of us have found it very difficult to forgive at some time in our lives. Some sins committed against us can bring deep emotional and psychological pain–and sometimes even physical pain. The motivation to get revenge can be very strong.

Forgiveness is particularly hard when we have been hurt by someone in a close relationship. But harboring vengeance in our hearts is more harmful to us than to the person we refuse to forgive. Thankfully, there is power to forgive when our focus is on how our Father has so graciously forgiven us through Jesus, rather than focusing on how someone has hurt us. May you know that healing power today.

Blessings, forgiven one, as you reflect forgiveness.

IN PRAYER

Lead Us Not Into Temptation

He will not let you be tested beyond your strength,
but with the testing he will also provide a way out
so that you may be able to endure it.

I Corinthians 10:13

We pray, "And lead us not into temptation."

Are you among those struggling with the meaning of this petition, wondering if it suggests that possibly God does lead some
people into temptation. Let's listen to Luther again. His explana-
tion in the Small Catechism can assist us in understanding this
petition as he tells us that God does not tempt anyone to sin, but
we pray that God would guard us so that the devil, the world, and
our sinful self may not lead us into sin, which he describes as false
belief, despair, and other great and shameful sins. And we pray
that when we are tempted God will give us the final victory.

This petition is the plea of conscious weakness, a cry of the soul
that admits vulnerability and prays that God will watch over us
and keep us from the tests that are too difficult for us. Isn't it good
that we can walk through the tests, trials, temptations of today
knowing that there is nothing that can separate us from God's
love?

Blessings as you rely on God's presence in your times of trial.

GLIMPSES OF GOD'S PRESENCE

Deliver Us

*Turn, O Lord, save my life; deliver me for the sake of
your steadfast love.*

Psalm 6:4

We pray, "But deliver us from evil."

Luther instructs us that here we pray that our heavenly Father would save us from every evil threatening body and soul, and at the time of our death would, by his grace, deliver us from the troubles of this world and bring us to himself in heaven.

Ah, yes, there are troubles in this world. We frequently hear the lament about how the wrong seems oft so strong. The newspapers and TV bombard us with stories of shootings, robberies, assaults, violence, war and other negative images. Whether it is true or not, we are led to believe that evil is more prevalent in society than it was in an earlier time. The literal Greek translation reads, "from the evil," which some say means "from the evil one." I certainly believe that there is an evil one whose finger is in the incidents of evil which we see around us.

But as followers of Jesus our attention is directed to the One who ultimately saves us from the evil one. We may suffer the consequences of evil events, but we know we have a loving Father who will be with us through the troubles of this world, and at last will take us to himself. Not much room for pessimism if we keep looking to Him.

Blessings as you trust God to deliver you from evil and from the evil one.

IN PRAYER

Amen

For in (Jesus) every one of God's promises is a "Yes."
For this reason it is through him we say the "Amen,"
to the glory of God.

II Corinthians 1:20

We pray, "For thine is the kingdom and the power and the glory forever and ever. Amen."

Again we turn to the Small Catechism where Luther explains that in saying "Amen" we are confident that God is pleased with such petitions and he hears them. After all, he has commanded us to pray them, and has promised to hear us.

Amen is a Hebrew word which has been transliterated into all modern languages in which Christians pray. It means "true" in the sense of "sure," "reliable," "valid." We close our prayers as a way of saying they are true and genuine, but also because we know God is true and reliable. It is a word of confidence in the God who loves us and has invited us to pray. It is a word which states we are sure that God hears our prayers, and though he will not always answer them in just the way we have prayed, he will answer in a way that is best for us.

We can count on God's presence and love for us today, because his word is sure. Amen!

Blessings as you trust in God who is true and reliable.

Adoration

Bless the Lord, O my soul. O Lord my God, you are very great. You are clothed with honor and majesty, wrapped in light as with a garment.

Psalm 104:1, 2

Way back in the days of my youth I learned an acronym which has been a helpful structure for my prayers through the years. It is a simple Bible reference: ACTS I. The next five reflections will be built on that prayer outline.

"A" stands for Adoration. It seems to me that it is appropriate to begin our prayers with a note of praising God for who he is as Creator, Savior, and Living Presence. If we begin our prayers with requests, we are turning in on ourselves. But when we begin with adoration we are opening ourselves up to God, rejoicing in his creative power, his holiness, his righteousness, and his loving care. It is a way of saying, "God, I love you, I respect you, I appreciate you, I honor you." I am convinced that life is better when our hearts are filled with adoration and praise. It's not that we will be richer, more successful, or spared the many trials that come with daily living, but life is better.

The Psalms can be a good teacher of this form of prayer, as they are filled with numerous examples. The shortest of them all (117) reads: "Praise the Lord, all you nations! Extol him, all you peoples! For great is his steadfast love toward us, and the faithfulness of the Lord endures for ever. Praise the Lord!"

Blessings as you praise God today.

IN PRAYER

Confession

I said, "I will confess my transgressions to the Lord,"
and you forgave the guilt of my sin.

Psalm 32:5

Today I would like to take a second look at the acronym which has been a helpful structure for my prayers: ACTS I.

"C" reminds us of confession. After we have offered our praise and adoration it is appropriate for us to confess our sin to God. Confession is the part of prayer which we would prefer to avoid. I know a pastor who is very reluctant to use the confession of sin which comes at the beginning of the Lutheran worship service because he does not want to offend people. Adam and Eve hid from God because they did not want to confess their disobedience, and many of us have excelled in following their example. Our culture avoids confession by disregarding the concepts of right and wrong.

When we avoid the confession of our sin we are trying to manufacture a god who is a warm, fuzzy creature of our imagination who overlooks our misdeeds. The God portrayed in the Scriptures is very different. Yes, he is loving and merciful, but he is also holy, righteous, and just.

The great blessing of confessing our sin is that it opens us up to hear the message of God's amazing grace. He answers our confession with the wonderful declaration that we are forgiven through Jesus. . . .we are made children of God through Jesus. . . .we are

85

GLIMPSES OF GOD'S PRESENCE

promised the presence of the Holy Spirit to help us journey through life in closer harmony with God who loves us. The pain of confession opens the door to the joy of forgiveness.

Blessings as you walk through the door of confession into the splendor of God's mercy.

IN PRAYER

Thanksgiving

O give thanks to the Lord, for he is good; for his steadfast love endures forever.

Psalm 106:1

Today I would like to take a third look at the acronym which has been a helpful structure for my prayers: ACTS I.

"T" reminds us of thanksgiving. When we have praised and adored God for who he is, and confessed to him who we are, we can joyfully thank him for what he has done. Quite naturally, the first bit of thanksgiving, after we have confessed our sin, would be for God's great promise of forgiveness and acceptance through Jesus. There are a host of other biblical promises, and of course there are the blessings of his providing and caring for us in our daily lives, all of which prompt us to give thanks. When we start to think of the beauty of creation with which he has surrounded us, the privilege of friendships, the marvelous way in which he created our bodies, we realize the list is just beginning, and we could spend hours thanking God.

As we read the Scriptures we sense that thanksgiving is a prominent theme for the people of God. "O give thanks to the Lord, call on his name, make known his deeds among the peoples. Sing to him, sing praises to him, tell of all his wonderful works" (I Chron. 16:8-10).

I am convinced that our lives are made better and happier as we grow in a spirit of gratitude, learning more and more to say, "Thank you," to God and to those around us.

Blessings as your prayers are filled with thanksgiving.

GLIMPSES OF GOD'S PRESENCE

Supplication

Do not worry about anything, but in everything by prayer and supplication with thanksgiving let your requests be made known to God.

Philippians 4:6

Today I would like to take a fourth look at the acronym which has been a helpful structure for my prayers: ACTS I.

"S" reminds us of supplication. When we have adored God for who he is, confessed our sin to him, and given thanks for what he has done, we begin with our personal requests.

Most of the time when I hear people talking about prayer they make mention of what they have asked God for rather than talking about their praise or thanksgiving. Yes, God wants us to come with our requests, but to me it seems that the more mature prayer pattern follows the ACTS format, with time given for praise, confession and thanksgiving before we start asking. Please understand that I am referring to the general pattern of our prayers, and not to the emergency "Help!" call, or the cries of the anguished and distressed soul.

Jesus has said, "Ask, and it will be given you....For everyone who asks receives" (Matt. 7:7,8). "Until now you have not asked for anything in my name. Ask and you will receive, so that your joy may be complete" (John 16:24). This does not mean that we can simply use God as an errand boy to cater to our whims. Certainly our requests would have to be in harmony with God's will.

IN PRAYER

How wonderful to know that God invites and encourages our prayers, even those in which we ask for personal blessings. Perhaps the first request should be for the guidance of his Spirit, so that we may know how to ask rightly.

Blessings in your prayers.

GLIMPSES OF GOD'S PRESENCE

Intercession

Pray for one another, so that you may be healed. The
prayer of the righteous is powerful and effective.
James 5:16

I would like to take a final look at the acronym which has been a helpful structure for my prayers: ACTS I.

"I" is the Roman numeral for one. As a letter in this acronym it stands for intercession. In our prayer life we are encouraged to look beyond our own needs to include the needs of others.

We don't understand how our prayers for others can benefit them, but the repeated testimony of people is that they are sure they have been helped through the prayers of others. While intercessory prayer was for many years dismissed by the scientific community as of no value, recent research has indicated that people in hospitals who have wide prayer support do better than those who have no prayer support. Those who are the prayer chain warriors in our churches have been confident of the value of intercessory prayer for a long time.

Intercessory prayer is not to be limited to our immediate friends and acquaintances. Our leaders, whether in church or government, need our prayer support, as well as hurting, grieving, suffering people around the world. The evening news could become a spiritual experience for us if we would use it as a prayer prompter

IN PRAYER

for all the people and problems which are brought to our attention. Jesus stretches the boundaries of intercessory prayer as he tells us to pray for those who persecute us (Matt.5:44). Who benefits from our intercessory prayer? I am convinced it is not only those for whom we pray, but also we who pray.

Blessings as you reach out to others in your prayers.

God's Presence In Our Scattered Thoughts

IN OUR SCATTERED THOUGHTS

Upside Down

Since, in the wisdom of God, the world did not know God through wisdom, God decided through the foolishness of our proclamation, to save those who believe.

I Corinthians 1:21

Once when Marilyn and I were visiting our daughter and her family I observed our five-year-old granddaughter watching a program on TV while standing on her head on the sofa, her back resting on the back of the sofa and her feet up against the wall. Perhaps that would be a better way to watch some of what is on TV.

The incident reminded me of the story in Acts 17 when some of Paul's and Silas's opponents complained to the city authorities about them, "These people who have been turning the world upside down have come here also." Some of us are convinced that the world was upside down and Paul came with a message to set it right. One of the reasons Jesus was crucified was because he challenged the current world perspective.

The upside down world says greatness is in being served, while Jesus said greatness is in serving. The upside down world says do whatever you can to gain power and control, even if it means tearing others down, while Jesus gives us the example of lifting others up. The world says there is great value in accumulating, while the Scriptures remind us it is more blessed to give than to receive. You can certainly think of other examples

GLIMPSES OF GOD'S PRESENCE

Followers of Jesus may appear, when judged by the standards of the world, to be standing on their heads, but maybe that is the way to see reality from God's perspective.

Blessings as you look at the world from God's perspective today.

IN OUR SCATTERED THOUGHTS

Examination of the Soul

My child, keep my words and store up my commandments with you; keep my commandments and live...write them on the tablet of your heart

Proverbs 7:1-3

A few minutes before conducting a wedding I usually say to the groom, "It is my practice to conduct an examination of the groom's sole before the wedding. Are you ready for that?" As a worried look begins to spread across the groom's face, I continue, "Show me the bottom of your shoe." A sample of what I have found is HOO on the left sole, and KED on the right. Of course, if I find something like that, I can conveniently forget to ask the couple to kneel during the service.

How would we feel if God were to say to us, "I want to conduct an examination of your soul"? What would he find written? Would it be negativism, fear, failure, sickness, self-centeredness, anger, greed, bitterness? Or would he find that we have let him hold our hand to write wholeness, love, generosity, forgiveness, thoughtfulness, kindness?

We may feel resistive to letting God conduct such an examination, but I am convinced that the only way to move toward wholeness is to regularly join him in that examination, and let him, through Jesus, clean away what does not belong there, and then guide our hand as we daily write what should be there.

Blessings in your soul writing.

97

GLIMPSES OF GOD'S PRESENCE

Robinson Crusoe Christians

If we walk in the light as he himself is in the light,
we have fellowship with one another.

I John 1:7

I can't say that I remember very many specifics from my seminary days, but one statement by Dr. George Aus lingers in my mind: "The New Testament does not know of any Robinson Crusoe Christians." He was emphasizing that the idea of Christians living in isolation from other Christians is not to be found in the New Testament. There is no hint of the validity of a person saying, "I can live out my faith by staying home, reading my Bible and praying, without any association with the Church." In Hebrews 10:24 it appears that some are trying to live independently, but it is discouraged as the author writes that we are not to neglect "to meet together, as is the habit of some."

To reach our fullest potential as followers of Jesus we need the encouragement and admonition of other followers–and they need ours. In the New Testament we see Christians who disagree with one another (sometimes very sharp differences), who are prejudiced, who snub others, who fail to show forgiveness, kindness, and thoughtfulness. Yet when, instead of going off to their own island they hang in there with other believers around the Word and Sacraments, the presence of the Living Lord helps them all to grow in faith and love.

I am thankful for the fellowship of believers who have encouraged me in my walk of faith. I affirm that statement of the Apostles'

98

IN OUR SCATTERED THOUGHTS

Creed, "I believe in the holy catholic Church, the communion of saints." I don't think I could have survived Robinson Crusoe style.

Blessings as you live in fellowship with other followers of Jesus.

GLIMPSES OF GOD'S PRESENCE

Who Will Win?

You did not choose me but I chose you. And I appointed you to go and bear fruit, fruit that will last.
John 15:16

Eyes all across the nation are focused on television sets on the evening of a presidential election. We wonder who will win. Will we be happy with the election results? Will it be good news or bad news in our opinion?

The good news is, YOU HAVE WON. God has voted for you. The deciding vote was cast on a cross and at an empty tomb nearly 2000 years ago. You have been chosen to occupy the heavenly mansion.

Some people want to maintain control of this election process, and think that the decisive vote is in their hands. They can choose for or against God. How wrong. God is King and Lord, no matter whether we vote for or against him. His vote is the only one which counts, and in Jesus he shows us that he votes for us. We, of course, can refuse to occupy the office. But the opportunity is there for us to gratefully accept it, and joyfully fulfill its responsibilities. As Luther reminds us in his Small Catechism, Jesus has redeemed us "with his holy and precious blood, and his innocent suffering and death....that I might be his own, live under him in his kingdom, and serve him in everlasting righteousness, innocence, and blessedness." What a privilege!

Blessings as you rejoice in God's decision to be FOR you, and as in gratitude you seek to bring honor and integrity into the office of son or daughter of the King.

Cataracts

Blessed are the eyes that see what you see!
Luke 10:23

"I can see the texture in the carpet!" "I can see the small pebbles on the ground!" "How thrilling to be able to see the distant trees so clearly!" Those are the kind of comments I heard from Marilyn during the few days following her cataract surgery. Through the years the lenses in her eyes gradually became more opaque, and objects were more difficult to see with clarity. Because of her surgeon's skill her sight was dramatically improved. She is excited about her restored vision.

There are ways in which our spiritual vision can easily become clouded so that we are unable to perceive spiritual realities with clarity. We may readily diagnose people whose behavior frequently causes problems for society as having an inability to see the significance of God's place in their lives, but is it possible for those of us who have the reputation of living more honorably to have spiritual cataracts? We who have experienced physical cataracts realize that the opaqueness develops so gradually that we are not really aware how much we have been missing until the problem is corrected through surgery. Then we are excited about our new found vision. I think there can be a parallel with spiritual sight and insight.

The Holy Spirit stands ready to use the instruments of Word and Sacraments to perform the surgery which enables us to see more

GLIMPSES OF GOD'S PRESENCE

clearly the reality of life in relationship with God, and with God's beloved people. As we entrust ourselves to his skillful work in us, we too may experience some moments of excitement in our spiritual lives.

Blessings as you let the Spirit of God correct your vision.

IN OUR SCATTERED THOUGHTS

Ringing the Bell

Your steadfast love is before my eyes, and I walk in faithfulness to you.

Psalm 26:3

During the funeral service for a good and faithful member of the church, a number of stories were shared about this man of faith. One woman told about how, some years earlier, she lived quite close to the church, but found more important things to do than worship on Sunday mornings. Each Sunday, at the time for the services to begin, she would hear the church bell being rung by the person whose life and faith we were remembering at the funeral service. Finally that bell beckoned her, and she started coming to church. Now she seldom misses a service, and in fact is the choir director.

The bell ringer probably never dreamed that what he was doing would have any appreciable consequences in anyone's life. He just kept ringing that bell every Sunday morning. But the Lord used that offering in an amazing way–somewhat like he used the boy's five loaves and two fish that the disciples thought were of no account. To me that is an encouraging word as we offer up our service to the Lord. Sometimes it may seem so small and insignificant, but when offered in faith to him, he may use it to bring blessings to someone in a way we can never imagine.

Blessings on you as you faithfully ring the bell the Lord has given to you.

103

GLIMPSES OF GOD'S PRESENCE

Walking in the Light

*I am the light of the world. Whoever follows me
will never walk in darkness, but will have the light
of life.*

John 8:12

Can you remember a time when you were particularly happy
to see the light? It happened for us on May 19, 1980, the morning after Mt. St. Helens erupted, spewing a cloud of ash which
increased the ground elevation at Ritzville, WA, more than
three inches. The ash cloud turned the sky black and by 1:00
PM on May 18 we were surrounded by the thickest darkness
I have ever seen. The cloud hovered over us the rest of the day,
but the next morning we awakened to a beautiful blue sky and
brilliant sunshine. When I mentioned seeing the light of that
morning in the next Sunday's sermon, faces throughout the
congregation beamed. We all sensed a new meaning of being in
the light.

The Bible uses the imagery of light and darkness to refer to spiritual realities. It speaks of being in the grips of sin and evil as walking in the darkness. But the good news is that God "has rescued us
from the power of darkness and transferred us into the kingdom
of his beloved Son" (Col. 1:13). Because we have been delivered
into light, we are called to walk in the light.

Walking in the light results in recognizing situations and circumstances which may cause us to stumble. Walking in the light

104

IN OUR SCATTERED THOUGHTS

means that we can see beyond our self-centered concerns and notice how we can bear one another's burdens and serve others. Jesus is the light who enables us to see the value of this way of life.

Blessings as you walk in the Light today.

GLIMPSES OF GOD'S PRESENCE

Finding the Clearing

*You show me the path of life. In your presence there
is fullness of joy.*

Psalm 16:11

Imagine yourself walking through a forest with majestic trees tow-
ering above you. Overhead there is a beautiful blue sky, and the
sunlight is filtering through the branches to cast intriguing light
and shadow patterns on the small plants growing at your feet.
You have left the trail to proceed toward a mountain lake where
you know there is excellent fishing. But the trees have hidden the
surrounding hills and mountains from your view, and knowing
how easy it is to begin walking in circles in this kind of situation,
you long for a clearing which will you enable to get your bearings
again.

Life is like walking through a forest. There is much that is lovely
and beautiful to observe as we move toward our ultimate goal.
But the trees of our daily tasks, obligations, friendships, and concerns can obscure the important landmarks and cause us to lose
our way. We need the clearings which will enable us to get our
bearings again.

God has provided clearings for us along the way. He calls us to
a place where we can see the eternal landmarks through reading and hearing his Word, and responding in prayer. He invites us
into the open spot of worship where we can gather around Word
and Sacraments and praise with other followers of Jesus. We find
a clearing as we reflect on how the activities of daily life relate

106

IN OUR SCATTERED THOUGHTS

to the grace and mercy of God shown in the crucified and risen Jesus. In these places we can understand where we are in relationship to where we are going, and then venture into the forest again.

Blessings as you seek out the clearings.

GLIMPSES OF GOD'S PRESENCE

Safe in God's Arms

*He will feed his flock like a shepherd; he will gather
the lambs in his arms, and carry them in his bosom.*
Isaiah 40:11

Not being accustomed to having a dog in the house I wasn't thinking about Charlie, our daughter's little beagle, when I opened the front door. In a flash, Charlie saw an opportunity to enjoy the outdoors, and darted past me. What a challenge to try to catch him! I knew that if I ran after him he would only run faster, so I walked at a quick pace, trying to keep him in sight as he explored a half dozen neighborhood yards.

I kept inviting Charlie to come to me, but to no avail. Then he darted around a corner and came upon a neighbor's open garage door. Being a beagle, he felt a compulsion to sniff everything inside while I remained outside talking with the neighbor. When I sensed Charlie had almost finished exploring the garage, I knelt down in the driveway and quietly called him to come to me, which he finally did.

What a parable of the human relationship with God. We may become so excited about sniffing out all the enticements of the world that we are lured into running away from God. If we feel that God is chasing us to punish us for escaping, we will probably try to avoid him. While we are running away he patiently keeps track of us and tenderly calls us to come to him. He knelt down to reach out for us in Jesus, and when we respond to his gracious invitation he lovingly sweeps us up in his strong arms to carry us safely home.

Blessings as you are loved and called by God.

IN OUR SCATTERED THOUGHTS

Y2K Power

You will receive power when the Holy Spirit has
come upon you, and you will be my witnesses.
Acts 1:8

There was much concern about power outages, loss of telephone service, and a host of other potential problems as the
calender rolled from 1999 to 2000. The predicted computer
glitches did not materialize, and we moved into the new year
with only a few minor troublesome incidents. But what the turn
of the year did not do, a violent windstorm did a day later as 800
homes in Spokane, WA, were without electrical power. Power
outages remind us of how dependent we have become upon
electricity.

There is another kind of power which we probably don't think
much about as the days go along smoothly, but which is abso-
lutely essential for our walk as followers of Jesus. As we read the
New Testament we see numerous references to that power of God
in the lives of people. The Evangelist Luke seems to be particularly cognizant of this power as he tells about the power of the
Lord being upon Jesus, and that same power active in the lives of
the disciples. People were impressed by the kind of power they
saw in the followers of Jesus–not power which sought to control people, but the power of faith which brought goodness and
healing.

Rejoice as you remember that the power of the Holy Spirit is
promised to you. There is power to make it possible for you to

109

GLIMPSES OF GOD'S PRESENCE

bring blessing, peace, healing, and joy to those around you. As we draw on this power we may not be turned into super persons, but we will be enabled to live honorably as faithful followers of Jesus.

Blessings as you are connected to the power.

IN OUR SCATTERED THOUGHTS

The One Who Strengthens Me

May you be made strong with all the strength that comes from his glorious power.

Colossians 1:11

Laura Wilkinson's hopes of being in the 2000 Olympic Games seemed shattered on March 8 when she hit her foot and fractured it in three places while practicing a dive. Early the next morning her coach knocked on her door and told her, "I don't care if your foot was cut off, you're diving in the Olympics." Within a few days she started climbing the ladder to the diving platform–wearing a cast. From there she rehearsed the dives in her mind, imagining the results. About three weeks before the Olympic trials she was finally able to get rid of the cast and get back into the water.

During the last five dives of the Olympic competition Laura rose from eighth place into first place. Then came the dangerous dive on which she had previously injured herself. She stood on the platform, 10 meters in the air, recalled her favorite Bible verse ("I can do all things through Christ, who strengthens me" (Phil. 4:13)), took the plunge and won the gold medal.

I am convinced that God does not take sides in sporting events, and Laura did not win simply because she thought of a Bible verse. But I am also convinced that her trust in Jesus gave her confidence and encouragement in the challenge which faced her. Each of us

111

GLIMPSES OF GOD'S PRESENCE

will also face plenty of challenges during the course of a lifetime. We can learn from Laura and receive the inner resources to meet those challenges by relying on the promise that the risen and living Lord is with us to strengthen us.

Blessings as you are strengthened by Christ today.

IN OUR SCATTERED THOUGHTS

When the Ground Shakes

We will not fear, though the earth should change,
though the mountains shake in the heart of the
sea; though its waters roar and foam, though the
mountains tremble with its tumult.

Psalm 46:2, 3

An earthquake? In Spokane? We will let Seattle and North Idaho have the earthquakes and we will be content to feel the distant ripple effects. Suddenly on June 25, 2001, we were jolted out of our complacency. Insignificant as it was as measured by other earthquakes, it did provide a topic of conversation.

The energy released by an earthquake is testimony to the awesome power of God who put this planet together and set it in place among all the stars, planets and moons in the vastness of the universe. If we pause long enough in our busy schedule to contemplate his creation we are humbled, put in our place, and filled with wonder. Are we not also prompted to praise and thank the Creator?

An even greater cause for wonder, though, is the fact that this almighty God even cares about us human beings, such infinitesimal specks in his vast universe. The Christian Gospel proclaims that he cares tremendously–enough to empty himself of his power, assume human flesh, and carry a cross to a hill outside Jerusalem. He is not a remote god, but remains intimately involved in our lives, attempting to reach out to draw us into the orbit of his

113

GLIMPSES OF GOD'S PRESENCE

amazing grace and love. Because of God's demonstration of love in Jesus, I know that I do not have to live in dread of the exhibitions of the Creator's power.

Blessings as God holds you firm in the shaking times of your life.

Abundant Water

Everyone who drinks of this water will be thirsty again, but those who drink of the water that I will give them will never be thirsty.

John 4:13-14

Water in abundance. That was our experience for three days as we watched two granddaughters participating in the Montana State swim meet. Water in the pool. Water out of the pool and splashed on me as I served as a timer. Water dripping from the participants. Yet, with all this water there was still the risk of dehydration, so numerous bottles of water were consumed by participants, cheering family members and officials.

While we were enjoying the water experience, a small plant at home was suffering from not receiving water during our absence. When we arrived home the leaves were withered and dried, causing us to wonder if there was still life in the plant. Fortunately, soaking the roots and some serious pruning revived it.

We, like the plant, need water for survival, both physically and in a spiritual sense. God has provided abundantly for our need. Psalm 1 speaks about the person who takes delight in the word of the Lord, saying that he or she is like a tree planted by streams of water. Jesus described himself as being the Living Water.

While I was timing some of the swimming events, a woman offered bottles of water to all of us timers. But she did not force us to

GLIMPSES OF GOD'S PRESENCE

drink. Similarly, God graciously offers us the Water of Life to keep us from spiritual dehydration, but he does not force us to accept. Wisdom gratefully and joyously receives the life-giving water, and finds ways to share it with those who are thirsty.

Blessings as you find refreshment and life in Jesus.

IN OUR SCATTERED THOUGHTS

Potato Chips

One does not live by bread alone, but by every word that comes from the mouth of God.
Matthew 4:4

A potato chip commercial stated, "Bet you can't eat just one." The implication is that they are so good you will want more. The negative side is that one won't satisfy you. A hundred won't satisfy you. Filling up on potato chips is not a healthy pastime. They taste good and create the desire for more, but they promise more than they can deliver.

The potato chip is symbolic of much in life: a craving for more is created, even though more cannot ultimately satisfy us. Think of some of life's potato chips:

Material goods: Those who have much want more. What is enough?

Power: Taste it, and it creates the desire for more. Power often corrupts.

Success: When is a person successful enough?

(Add your own chips.)

The prophet Isaiah poses an alternative for our potato chip culture: "Why do you spend your money for that which is not bread, and your labor for that which does not satisfy? Listen carefully to me,

117

GLIMPSES OF GOD'S PRESENCE

and eat what is good, and delight yourselves in rich food. Incline your ear, and come to me; listen so that you may live" (Is.55:2,3).

Jesus echoes the theme: "I am the bread of life: whoever comes to me will never be hungry, and he who believes in me will never be thirsty" (John 6:35).

Blessings on your eating.

Cats and Vets

If we confess our sins, he who is faithful and just will forgive our sins and cleanse us from all unrighteousness.

I John 1:9

Rupert Sheldrake, in his book *Dogs That Know When Their Owners are Coming Home,* writes about cats which somehow sense when their owners are planning to take them to the veterinarian, and they simply vanish. He carried out a survey of veterinary clinics in North London, asking whether some cat owners had cancelled appointments because their cats had gone into hiding. Sixty-four out of sixty-five clinics reported that it happened quite frequently. The sixty-fifth simply told owners to bring the cats in whenever they could. The owners knew that it would be beneficial to the cats' well being to have a visit with the vet, but try to convince the cats of that. They resisted the visit in every possible way.

Somehow those cats remind me of Adam and Eve hiding from God in the Garden of Eden. The best possible thing for them to have done would be to stop hiding behind their excuses and rationalizations, come out into the open to confess their disobedience which would open the door to receive forgiveness, and to be reconciled to their Creator. Instead, they hid. Have any of us acted the same way? Is there an impulse in us to avoid God when we know that we have brought guilt upon ourselves?

GLIMPSES OF GOD'S PRESENCE

The invitation of Jesus is, "Come to me....and you will find rest for your souls" (Matthew 11:28, 29). In the loving, caring presence of our Savior there is peace, rest and healing which will certainly escape us if we practice avoidance mechanisms.

Blessings as you are drawn to the Great Physician.

IN OUR SCATTERED THOUGHTS

Follow the Leader

Lay aside every weight and the sin which clings so closely, and let us run with perseverance the race that is set before us, looking to Jesus the pioneer and perfecter of our faith.

Hebrews 12:1, 2

Do you remember, as a child, playing the game "Follow the Leader"? Were you ever the leader, choosing to jump over a water puddle, run for fifty feet, reach up to touch a branch, and turn a somersault, while the other children imitated you? Imagine a child behind you who was distracted by a butterfly on a colorful flower, and just had to step out of line to observe it. There was also a puppy which just had to be petted. Those were interesting activities, but the child failed to accomplish the purpose of the game.

Jesus frequently called people to follow him. Following Jesus meant loyalty and a commitment to what he was doing as he went around Galilee proclaiming the Kingdom of God. It was an exhilarating experience to follow Jesus as the crowds thronged around him to hear him teach and to receive his healing touch. But it also became risky and frightening as the opposition mounted and he was led to the cross. Following had its reward in the joy of seeing the risen Jesus.

In his mercy and love Jesus calls us to follow him into the exciting adventure of the Kingdom of God. There will be times when

121

GLIMPSES OF GOD'S PRESENCE

following will be hard, but as we keep our eyes on Jesus we will discover that the Holy Spirit is with us to encourage and strengthen us in the endeavor, and we, too, will experience the joy which those early disciples knew in the presence of Jesus.

Blessings as you follow Jesus.

Temporary Falls

In the beginning... God created the heavens and the earth.

Genesis 1:1

Marilyn and I stood near Deception Falls, watching the Tye River rushing on its way to the sea, the foaming water tumbling over hidden rocks and sending a misty spray up into the air. We noticed an interpretive sign which declared that the falls were only temporary. The action of the water on the rocks would eventually wear them down and they would become mere rapids for the water to tumble over on its journey to the ocean. As we looked at the falls it seemed almost impossible to believe, but we realize that is the effect water has on rocks over the centuries.

The thought of "temporary" waterfalls made me stand in awe of God who put the processes of nature in place to create mountains, rivers and oceans. I recalled the words of the Psalmist, "Lord, you have been our dwelling place in all generations. Before the mountains were brought forth, or ever you had formed the earth and the world, from everlasting to everlasting you are God" (Psalm 90:1-2). I coupled that with another repeated affirmation of the Psalms: "The steadfast love of the Lord endures forever." Even if we cannot count on rocks to withstand the abrasive effect of water, we can trust that God endures forever, and his steadfast love will never fail. That should give us reason to rejoice in this day which the Lord has made.

Blessings as the eternally dependable God holds you firm in faith.

Perspective Through Worship

*O come, let us worship and bow down, let us kneel
before the Lord, our Maker.*

Psalm 95:6

Why is it that evil people often seem to prosper, while many good people have such a struggle? We are perplexed as we see people who have no regard for God, nor concern for others, accumulate wealth and power enabling them to live in luxury and ease, while many good, honest, righteous people face poverty, hardship, and illness. It doesn't seem right.

An ancient psalmist struggled with the same questions in Psalm 73. He wrote, "I was envious of the arrogant; I saw the prosperity of the wicked." He describes their smugness as they are convinced they can pull the wool over God's eyes saying, "How can God know? Is there knowledge in the Most High?" The Psalmist describes his perplexity as he writes, "But when I thought how to understand this, it seemed to me a wearisome task." Insight came when "I went into the sanctuary of God."

Like the Psalmist we are confronted by a host of unanswerable questions. There is much in life which does not seem right and fair. But we have discovered, as he discovered, participating in worship gives perspective. It is not that we are handed the answers to all our questions, but we are given a faith to live through all situa-

IN OUR SCATTERED THOUGHTS

tions. God comes to us to assure us that no matter what happens in life we are held in his loving arms. In his care we have riches which those who have no regard for God will never know, and they are the kind of riches which last into eternity.

Blessings as your life is enriched through worship.

GLIMPSES OF GOD'S PRESENCE

An Encouraging Word

*I commend you to God and to the message of his
grace, a message that is able to build you up.*
Acts 20:32

Julie anticipated her year of internship with excitement as she looked forward to developing her skills in parish ministry. Discouragement soon set in because she never heard a word of commendation from her supervising pastor who was quick to point out her weaknesses and mistakes. She was beginning to believe she wasn't doing much of anything right. In her final evaluation at the end of the year he told her she was the best intern he had ever worked with. She wondered why some of that encouragement could not have been spread throughout the year.

I wonder how many of us have felt like Julie as we have heard discouraging and critical words. There are probably times when we need to have some faults pointed out in the spirit of love, but, oh, how we need to hear words which inspire, build us up and motivate us to do our very best. I am grateful for the people who have spoken such words to me.

God speaks the most powerfully encouraging words as he reminds us that we are precious in his sight. Jesus, the Living Word, has brought us a strong message of love and grace. As that message sinks into our hearts we can deal with the dispiriting words which come our way. When we are caught up in the wonder of that message we discover it has a marvellous way of shaping our words, so that they become grace-filled words which build others up.

Blessings as God's word of grace shapes your words.

IN OUR SCATTERED THOUGHTS

Seeing Ourselves

*The word of God is living and active...it is able to
judge the thoughts and intentions of the heart.*
Hebrews 4:12

A cute four and a half year old Korean girl greeted me with a smile. Her adoptive mother told me about bringing the little tyke from Korea when she was four months old. Most of the other children she has known have been Caucasians, but recently her parents had her in a group where all the children were Asian. Afterward she commented, "Mommy, those children were different. Their eyes were different."

Do we sometimes have difficulty seeing ourselves as we really are? Do you suppose God ever chuckles over our self perceptions? Maybe there are times when he cries. Like those old fun house mirrors with unusual curvatures reflecting very strange images back to us, there are folk religion mirrors which reflect distorted spiritual images.

The Word of God is a mirror which portrays a true likeness, giving two distinct images. The first is one that I would prefer not to look at as it indicts every one of us. We are reminded that we have fallen from the image of God in which we were created. Thank God, there is a second image–that of people who are dearly loved by God. Through Jesus he forgives, declares us innocent, and claims us as his beloved children. When the reality of his amazing grace sinks into our skulls we will want to say a "Hallelujah!" or two. As we let the Scriptures hold these two images in tension before us, we will begin to see ourselves more clearly as we truly are.

Blessings as you look into the mirror of God's Word.

127

GLIMPSES OF GOD'S PRESENCE

When Disaster Becomes Beauty

We also boast in our sufferings, knowing that suffering produces...character and character produces hope.

Romans 5:3-4

Driving through Kootenai, Banff, and Glacier Parks I was struck anew by the beauty of the Rocky Mountains. The sunshine glistened on the first snowfall of the year, brightening the rugged peaks and highlighting the evergreens on the lower slopes. I was impressed again by the layered lines of stone exposed in the sheer cliffs, some of them in a horizontal pattern, but others almost vertical. I was reminded that those mountains were once below sea level, and the layers had been formed by centuries of accumulation on the ocean floor. They were thrust up into their present patterns as the tectonic plates moved against one another. The tremendous earthquakes produced by the slipping of those moving plates would be declared disasters if they were to happen today. But now we gaze at the results and marvel, "What wondrous beauty!"

Those mountains remind me of some people I have known. These people have experienced pressures and "earthquakes" in their lives, and have risen from them as beautiful people, demonstrating an exceptional attitude toward their adversities and losses.

True to his promise that he works for good in everything to those who love him, God has a remarkable way of transforming tragic and evil events. Even a horrible crucifixion became the avenue

128

IN OUR SCATTERED THOUGHTS

of forgiveness and eternal salvation for sinful humanity. Trusting the promise of his presence, we allow him to work through the pressured times to create in us wondrous layers of strength and beauty. As followers of Jesus we dare to trust that promise in the days of crisis.

Blessings as you trust God through the days of your personal earthquakes.

I'd Rather Have You

You are a chosen race, a royal priesthood, a holy nation, God's own people.

I Peter 2:9

Following one of the daily chapel services at the Good Samaritan retirement and nursing home, I took my usual place at the rear of the chapel to greet the residents as they left the service. A ninety-year-old woman wheeled her chair up to me and I said, "The Lord be with you." She responded, "Honey, I'd rather have you." Wow! Some people really make bad choices.

How many times in our lives have we wanted some other person, thing, or attitude rather than the presence of the Lord? "I want to manage my finances the way I choose, rather than having the Lord as my financial consultant." "I know my association with this person tends to pull me away from God, but I enjoy him (her) so much that I want to continue to be with him (her)." "I want to read this fascinating book rather than find time for the Bible and prayer."

I have no doubt God can find more interesting, more devout, more lovable people to be around than me (and possibly you), but the wonder is that he wants us to be a part of his eternal company. He honored us with his presence as he came to live among us in Jesus. He invites us to come to him, to be with him, to know peace and joy in his presence as they can be found nowhere else. It could be argued that God made a bad choice in wanting to be with us, but I am certainly thankful that he made that decision.

Blessings as you rejoice in God's decision for you.

Word of Blessing

For God has destined us not for wrath, but for obtaining salvation through our Lord Jesus Christ, who died for us so that...we may live with him. Therefore encourage one another and build up each other, as indeed you are doing."

I Thessalonians 5:9-11

In his book *Grateful Living* Dale Turner writes about Alice Freeman Potter, a former president of Wellesley College, teaching a Sunday School class composed of young girls from a city slum. It was not a very promising group. There was no resemblance to the freshly scrubbed, well-dressed, bright-eyed children she knew from suburban churches. One Sunday she instructed them, "Find something beautiful in your home, and tell me about it next Sunday." One girl came back with the report, "There's nothing beautiful except the sunshine on our baby's curls."

Years later, after that youngster had grown to become a woman with significant accomplishments, she reflected that her teacher's challenge changed her way of thinking and her way of life. As she started to look for the beautiful she began to catch glimpses of it in her surroundings and in herself.

I doubt Alice Potter ever expected such a significant result from those few words. Others have also been surprised to hear that their words, spoken years earlier, had great effect. Perhaps you also have had the privilege of being thanked for words which

GLIMPSES OF GOD'S PRESENCE

have blessed. As we hear and respond to God's gracious, mercy-filled words to us, we are led to speak to others with words shaped by his love. Those words go out with power to heal, to encourage, to comfort, and to give hope.

Blessings as your words deliver the goodness of God to others.

IN OUR SCATTERED THOUGHTS

Worshiping the Divine Majesty

Extol the Lord our God; worship at his footstool.
Holy is he!

Psalm 99:5

As Marilyn and I were worshiping with a congregation in another city we came to the time for the prayer of the day. We all prayed together, "By your Spirit enable us so to worship our divine majesty...." Suddenly I realized the horrible words which we had spoken—words which claimed for ourselves that which belongs to God alone. I am sure it was a simple typographical error which should have read, "your divine majesty." But we prayed that we might worship *our* divine majesty.

I began to wonder how often what we had so blatantly done in that prayer is worked out in the course of our daily living. We sometimes use the expression "playing God" in describing people claiming too much authority or prestige for themselves. Playing God began with Adam and Eve as they chose to disobey the command of God. It continues with us whenever we put our self-centered interests ahead of God's good and holy will for our lives. We, in effect, put ourselves at the center of our universe, usurping the place that belongs to God. We worship "our divine majesty," usually without even realizing it.

The good news is that God continues to love us, in spite of our attempts to nudge him off the throne. He has shown his amazing love through the cross of Calvary. He offers us forgiveness

133

GLIMPSES OF GOD'S PRESENCE

through Jesus, and he sends his Holy Spirit to inspire in us a spirit of gratitude and love which enables us to worship God's divine majesty and praise his glorious name.

Blessings as you give thanks and praise God today.

IN OUR SCATTERED THOUGHTS

The Address

Do not let your hearts be troubled....In my Father's house there are many dwelling places....And if I go and prepare a place for you, I will come again and will take you to myself, so that where I am, there you may be also.

John 14:1-3

"We certainly will miss him, but we know what his address is," a woman commented, reflecting on the death of her 56-year-old husband. In the memorial service sermon the pastor, focusing on the words, "Let not your hearts be troubled," commented that there certainly is reason for sorrow and grief at the time of the death of a loved one, but there is no reason for worry, anxiety, and fear, because of the resurrection of Jesus. We have a living Lord who died and rose again for us. The promises of God are made certain for his people through Jesus.

Marilyn reflected the next morning about two widows we have known. Both of them lost their husbands very suddenly at about the same age. The one referred to above, living with the assurance of the promises of Jesus, was dealing well with her loss. The other one has had a terrible time. She and her husband had not made the promises of Jesus a core part of their lives.

Our heavenly Father loves us dearly. He wants us to be able to walk through all the experiences of living and dying strengthened and encouraged by his promises. He wants us to know that death is not the end for our loved ones or for us. There is a living Lord and Savior who has an address ready for us.

Blessings as you let him deliver you from a troubled heart.

135

GLIMPSES OF GOD'S PRESENCE

Your Rocks Are Beautiful

Who is a rock besides our God?

Psalm 18:31

The Spokane River flow is high in May and June as the melting snow from the mountains trickles down through countless rivulets to merge in the river on its way to the ocean. As it flows through downtown Spokane, the river cascades over the Spokane Falls, sending spray high into the air.

Later in the summer the river settles down to a lesser flow, most of which is channeled through a power plant. A woman told me of a "later in the summer" incident in 1974, the summer Spokane hosted a world's fair. The woman struck up a conversation with a woman from China as they were viewing the nearly dry falls. She remarked that she wished the tourist could have been here earlier to see the beauty of the abundant water pouring over the falls. The Chinese woman remarked, "I think your rocks are beautiful." And she was right.

We sometimes become so enthralled with the spectacular that we pay less attention to the commonplace. There are times when the commonplace is as important as the spectacular. I have seen it in churches. Some people stand out and make wonderful contributions to congregational life. I thank God for them. I have also learned to see the beauty of some ordinary people who, rock solid in their faith, contribute mightily to the life of the Church in less spectacular ways. I thank God for them.

IN OUR SCATTERED THOUGHTS

I can't think of any place in the Scriptures where God is compared to a waterfall, but there are many places where he is likened to a rock–a solid foundation for our faith.

Blessings as your life is grounded on the Rock of Ages.

GLIMPSES OF GOD'S PRESENCE

Spirit Formed Lives

Do not be conformed to this world, but be transformed by the renewing of your minds.

Romans 12:2

"Mommy, I want God to do for me what he's done for Daddy." I read those words in one of our daughter's books while I was in their home several years ago. They are the words of the five-year-old daughter of Lee Strobel, appearing in his book *The Case for Christ*. Strobel describes himself as an atheist who was profane, angry, verbally harsh, drunken, self-absorbed, a liar, and a cheater. He was disturbed when his wife became a Christian, but after a while he noticed some remarkable changes in her. He became intrigued about what might lie behind those changes. As a hard-nosed reporter who had spent much time covering court cases, he decided to apply the investigative procedures and evidence requirements of criminal courts to determine what the evidence was for the validity of Christianity. After nearly two years of extensive investigation, he came to the conclusion that the evidence pointing to Jesus as the Son of God was much more compelling than the evidence for atheism. He knew he had to decide on the basis of the evidence, and made the commitment to follow Jesus. In a few months his little daughter had noticed the difference.

So it is when we associate with Jesus. For some the life changes are sudden and dramatic. For others the shaping is more gradual over time. I thank God for Jesus who is alive and sends his Spirit to form our lives more closely to the image God originally intended for us.

Blessings as you let the Spirit do his work in you.

Rooted

As therefore you have received Christ Jesus the Lord, continue to live your lives in him, rooted and built up in him and established in the faith, just as you were taught, abounding in thanksgiving.

Colossians 2:6, 7

One evening when we were enjoying a corn feed at the home of some friends, the hostess talked with me about how she enjoys working in her garden, and how it becomes a spiritual experience for her. She is a Word and Sacrament Christian who knows that the spiritual life needs to be nurtured by more than merely communing with nature. But being out in her garden gives her opportunity to reflect on her relationship with God.

She spoke about pulling weeds, and thinking about being rooted. A weed with its roots pulled out of the soil cannot continue living. And she commented that it is the same in regard to our spiritual lives. We must continually be receiving the nourishment which comes through being firmly rooted in God's grace.

There are enemies, both "out there" and inside us, which would like to yank our roots out of the rich soil of God's grace where we are nourished though his Word and Sacraments. And so we pray, "Deliver us from evil," and trust that God will keep us in his grace.

Blessings as your roots sink deeply into God's grace.

GLIMPSES OF GOD'S PRESENCE

Loss as a Lens

We know that in all things God works for good for those who love God.

Romans 8:28

There was a mixture of sadness and joy as Marilyn and I drove home after taking our daughter to begin her first year at Pacific Lutheran University. We were happy for her, but we also felt loss because we knew that life in our home would not be the same without her. We would miss her deeply. After we arrived home and Marilyn was cleaning the bathroom, the sight of Cheryl's blonde hairs triggered her emotions.

After the tears stopped flowing, Marilyn looked out the back door and saw a young woman struggling to walk up the alley. Some years before this woman had been a bright and capable young person, but a tragic automobile accident left her with injuries to her brain and body. There was no possibility of her going to college or holding a job through which she could support herself. Marilyn's sense of loss was suddenly put into perspective. Cheryl had been given to us so we could help her prepare to fly. We could now rejoice that we had been able to accomplish that, and she was fully capable of leaving the nest.

Losses in life can sometimes become the lens through which we may see our purpose in life and discover what is of most value. Losses are never fun, but we have the promise that God is with

IN OUR SCATTERED THOUGHTS

us in the midst of them. If, at those times, we look to him and the promise of his grace rather than looking to ourselves in self pity, we will grow in grace through the difficulties.

Blessings as you rely on the God of all comfort in your losses.

GLIMPSES OF GOD'S PRESENCE

Carried to the Summit

For by grace you have been saved through faith,
and this is not your own doing.

Ephesians 2:8

In the summer of 2000 the first paraplegic climber reached the top of Mt. Rainier using a self-designed, hand-cranked "snow pod." In 2001 the first blind man reached the summit of Mt. Everest. What remarkable achievements! It seems that almost anything is possible these days.

Almost.

One thing is, and always will be, beyond human ability: being able to climb the mountain of eternal life. To reach that height we need to be carried in strong arms. Popular theology claims that we can make it on our own. I don't know how many times at funerals I have heard a statement to the effect, "He was such a good man. He certainly deserves to go to heaven." The problem with this popular theology is that it is in sharp contrast with God's revelation in Jesus. The strong affirmation of the Scripture is that "'No human being will be justified in his (God's) sight' by deeds prescribed by the law" (Romans 3:20). When we begin to understand the holiness of God we begin to realize the hopelessness of the human condition.

The amazing message of the Christian faith is that God is not willing to let us remain in hopelessness, but in Jesus he has provided the strong arms to carry us to the summit. The arms that

142

IN OUR SCATTERED THOUGHTS

accepted human weakness and were stretched out on the cross have, through the power of God, become the arms of our deliverance. In gratitude we are moved to strive harder than ever to live a good life.

Blessings as you give thanks for being carried in those strong arms.

GLIMPSES OF GOD'S PRESENCE

Time to Sweep the Tent

Hear the word of the Lord, all you people.
Jeremiah 7:2

One Sunday morning while camping Marilyn and I put on some nicer clothes to go into town for a church service. I wandered away from the camp site while Marilyn was fixing breakfast. When I came back, I entered the tent with the intention of sweeping it, since the abundant sand seemed to excel in finding its way inside. Surprised to find it so clean I called out, "Marilyn, did you sweep the tent?" She called back , "No, and I'm not going to while I have these clothes on." Obviously there was some miscommunication, which was quickly resolved as I exlained that I was not implying that she should, but was just surprised that it was so clean. Since then we have often used the words, "It's time to sweep the tent," when one of us has perceived a communication lapse.

Does the tent need sweeping in our understanding of what God is trying to communicate to us? Sometimes God has a hard time getting through to us. He has tried through coming as Jesus, whom the Gospel of John describes as the Word of God (John 1:1-14). He is God's ultimate message to us, and as we try to pay close attention to that Word, we will be begin to understand more of what God is saying to us.

And I begin to wonder: as we hear the voice of God more clearly through Jesus, the Word, won't we also be able to listen more closely, and with more love and concern, to those around us so that less sand will be tracked into our human relationships, making tent sweeping a lot easier?

Blessings in your tent sweeping.

144

IN OUR SCATTERED THOUGHTS

An Inestimable Treasure

*The kingdom of heaven is like a merchant in search
of fine pearls; on finding one pearl of great value,
he went and sold all that he had and bought it.*
Matthew 13:45-46

Marilyn received a phone call from someone soliciting money for
a fund to assist firemen, including such things as buying equipment for them. If we would make a contribution, the caller promised to send us a packet of information which we could "keep for
yourselves, share with a friend, or use to line your bird cage, as I
do." That did not sound like a very convincing solicitation pitch.

Can you imagine what the spread of Christianity would have been
like if Paul, Peter, James, John, and the rest of the early followers of
Jesus had a similar estimate of the value of the Gospel (the good
news of God's amazing love through Jesus)? If that had been the
case, probably none of us would ever have heard of Jesus. Thank
God, they spread the news with tremendous conviction.

The incident prompts some introspective questions: Have I at
times made the Gospel seem like something of little value:

through lack of enthusiasm in sharing?

through failure to demonstrate that it has much power to affect
attitudes and behavior?

through withholding gratitude and praise?

The good news of Jesus is an inestimable treasure, not to be
locked away in some safe deposit box, but to be lived and shared.

145

GLIMPSES OF GOD'S PRESENCE

A part of that good news is that even when the answers to the introspective questions accuse us, God continues to love us, forgive us, and send his Spirit to help us grow as his children.

Blessings as you rejoice in the Gospel.

Follow Me

*My sheep hear my voice. I know them, and they
follow me. I give them eternal life.*

John 10:27-28

Noticing the puzzled look on my face as he was giving me somewhat complicated directions to an unfamiliar location, my friend finally said, "Oh, just follow me." It was very easy to reach the destination when I simply followed.

The expression, "Follow me," as it came from Jesus's lips, must have made quite an impression on the Gospel writers. It appears twenty times in the four gospels. Jesus does not require knowing all the ins and outs of theology, or having a resume which includes holding several major offices in a congregation, as prerequisites for eternal life. He never told anyone that they had to measure up to a perfect moral standard to qualify for a place in the heavenly mansion. He simply says, "Follow me."

The prospect of following Jesus may seem to be both very risky, and the safest thing to do. In the Gospels we read about some who became antagonists of Jesus as they perceived him as a threat to their status, power, control and self-interest. Others found safety in the promises of Jesus that they would never perish, and no one would ever snatch them out of his hand.

As we are confronted by this tension between risk and safety, Jesus reaches out to us saying, "Follow me." In following we are

GLIMPSES OF GOD'S PRESENCE

surprised by joy (C. S. Lewis), amazed by grace (John Newton), captivated by being loved (Apostle John), and empowered by Christ living in us (Apostle Paul).

Blessings as you follow Jesus.

The Wounded Blossom

Each of us must please our neighbor for the good purpose of building up the neighbor.
                                                      Romans 15:2

Marilyn and I were the recipients of a lovely fall flower bouquet. We enjoyed it for several days, but as the blossoms wilted it became time to throw them away. One of the longest lasting flowers was a carnation. What a surprise when Marilyn pulled it out and discovered that the stem had been damaged just below the bud so that the flower folded down as soon as it was pulled away from the supporting flowers around it. It was able to draw enough moisture through the wounded stem to be sustained, but it could certainly not stand tall by itself.

That bouquet reminded us of what the fellowship of believers should and can be. The Scriptures encourage followers of Jesus to build one another up and to encourage each other. Many have found that when they have been wounded in body or spirit, they have been upheld by other followers of Jesus who have prayed for them, listened to them, encouraged them, and supported them. I am grateful for what I am privileged to see of that ongoing ministry in the life of the Church.

Our Lord calls us to be the flowers in his bouquet which help some of the wounded ones to keep their heads high, but also to be willing to receive the support of others when we are the wounded ones.

Blessings as you are part of the supporting fellowship.

GLIMPSES OF GOD'S PRESENCE

Body Parts

*Now you are the Body of Christ and individually
members of it.*

I Corinthians 12:27

In a weekly Bible study a group of ninth grade students were
focusing on biblical images of what it means to be the Church.
One evening while studying I Corinthians 12, which describes
the Church as the Body of Christ, I asked them which body part
best described their function in the church. One who was a gifted
speaker replied, "I am the tongue." Another described himself as
an ear. So it went around the group until one person said, "I am
the colon." None of us expected anyone to take pride in being that
part of the body, but then we remembered that his first name was
Colin.

The statement underscored the meaning of Paul's statement, "...
the members of the body that seem to be weaker are indispens-
able, and those members of the body that we think less honorable
we clothe with greater honor....But God has so arranged the body,
giving the greater honor to the inferior member, that there may
be no dissension within the body, but the members may have the
same care for one another" (I Corinthians 12:22-25).

Do we sometimes get things mixed up in the life of the Church,
giving greater honor to those who do the public work of the
Church, while overlooking those quiet ones who do the undesir-
able (perhaps more important) servant work?

150

IN OUR SCATTERED THOUGHTS

Whatever part of the body you would choose to describe your function in the Church, you are an important part of the Body as God has given you gifts to help the Body function in a healthy way.

Blessings as you use your gifts for the health of the Body.

GLIMPSES OF GOD'S PRESENCE

Access

Through (Jesus) we have obtained access to this grace in which we stand; and we boast in our hope of sharing the glory of God.

Romans 5:2

Two yellow cards–each the size of a credit card. One displayed Marilyn's picture and name, the other mine. Both of them had the words "ESCORT REQUIRED" printed on them. The name of the approved escort (our son-in-law) was also printed on the card.

Our son-in-law is stationed at the Pentagon and has access to many parts of that huge building. Marilyn and I, of course, had no access apart from him. I can just imagine walking up to that building and saying to the guards, "I am private citizen Duane Ul-leland, and I plan to wander inside and look around." They would either have laughed at me or arrested me. But with our son-in-law we were able to walk into many places in the building, sometimes through some very non-public and unattractive service areas, down long hallways (some having semicircular blue carpets in front of doorways signifying the offices of generals), and into his office.

The experience reminded me of the One who said, "I am the way, and the truth, and the life. No one comes to the Father except through me." Walking through the Pentagon was a privilege not to be taken lightly, but it pales in comparison to the gift of being ushered into the eternal presence of God. A visit to the Pentagon

IN OUR SCATTERED THOUGHTS

was a once in a lifetime experience, but the promise of the presence of God is a daily reality. It is with joy and gratitude that we accept the access given by Jesus.

Blessings as you marvel at the access provided by Jesus.

GLIMPSES OF GOD'S PRESENCE

Does God Have Your Number?

Can a woman forget her nursing child, or show no compassion for the child of her womb? Even these may forget, yet I will not forget you. See, I have inscribed you on the palms of my hands.

Isaiah 49:15, 16

Have you ever received the impression that your number is more important than you are? In a telephone transaction in which I could not get by just giving my name, a woman asked for my account number, and my zip code as well. Frequently we are asked for our Social Security number in some business dealing. Oh, and also that credit card number, as well as telephone, street, bank account and birth date numbers. In contrast, read Isaiah 43:1 which portrays God as saying, "Do not fear, for I have redeemed you; I have called you by name, you are mine." These words were directed to the nation of Israel, but they reflect the character of a knowing, loving, caring God.

There is no indication we are merely a number in a heavenly computer. Jesus reveals to us a loving Father who governs our world– not one who is far removed from us, but one who cares for us as individuals. His love for us is personal, and we are not lost in a sea of humanity. The most powerful demonstration of that love took place on a cross. How good it is to know in times of trial, struggle, betrayal and oppression, as well as in times of joy and celebration, that we have a loving Father who cares about us. As we live in what is so often an uncaring and impersonal world, God loves us.

Blessings as you are upheld by the love of God.

Warning

Let your heart hold fast my words; keep my commandments and live.

Proverbs 4:4

A manufacturer's warning on a power drill stated, "Not intended for use as a dental drill." Another manufacturer felt a need to alert purchasers of a children's scooter, "This product moves when used." The label on a set of shin pads read, "Shin pads cannot protect any part of the body they do not cover."

Most of us have probably purchased products with similar warnings that have left us wondering just how stupid the manufacturers think we are. Apparently they have experienced a number of situations where consumers have used products in very strange ways, and then have sued the manufacturer. Do you suppose that is why God put a few "Thou shalt nots" in the Bible? Did he anticipate some really stupid behavior on the part of human beings as we live out our relationship with him, with other human beings, and with our environment? Did he possibly foresee that he would be blamed when our behavior resulted in disastrous consequences?

I believe that God has given us commandments ("Do this" as well as "Don't do that"), not to restrict our freedom, but as an expression of his love and his concern that life will be good for us. Unfortunately, each of us has demonstrated our lack of attentiveness to his commands, and consequently has taken some of the goodness out of life for ourselves and for others. As that happens,

GLIMPSES OF GOD'S PRESENCE

may God grant us the wisdom to turn to him in repentance, receive his forgiveness, and accept the guidance of his Spirit to help us experience the joy of obedience.

Blessings in your use of God's good gifts.

IN OUR SCATTERED THOUGHTS

The Numbers Praise God

*The heavens are telling the glory of God; and the
firmament proclaims his handiwork.*
                                          Psalm 19:1

During a Monday morning conversation, a woman told Marilyn
and me that she had not looked forward to the mathematics class
she was required to take as she was working toward a degree.
She anticipated that it would be a boring encounter with a series
of numbers. She was delightfully surprised when the professor
at Whitworth College, a Presbyterian-related school in Spokane,
began to speak about mathematics as an expression of the wonderful world God created. Math bears testimony to the order in
God's creation. For the professor it was not only angels and arch-
angels who give glory to God. Numbers and mathematical equa-
tions join in the paean of praise. It was fun to see the glimmer in
the lady's eyes as she shared this insight.

I had never thought about numbers praising God as I balanced
my checkbook, but I probably will in the future. Thank God, he did
build some numerical sense into this world, enabling us to deal
with check books and banking systems. His gift of mathematics
makes possible the more complicated aspects of science and
physics in the universe as well. How would we ever get satellites
into orbit if God had not excelled at math? I thank God for con-
versations like Monday's which can help open my eyes to see the
glory of God in the common things of life–even numbers.

Blessings as you join the numbers in praising God.

157

The Gestures

And whatever you do, in word or deed, do everything in the name of the Lord Jesus, giving thanks to God the Father through him.

Colossians 3:17

There are some among us who cannot talk without using our hands. A friend told me about one such pastor who was gesturing energetically while speaking to his congregation, with the message being interpreted through sign language. Suddenly some of the hearing impaired persons burst into laughter, and the pastor paused, with a puzzled look on his face. He did not think he had said anything funny. The interpreter walked over to him, pinned the pastor's arms to his side, and said, "Keep your hands at your side. You do not know what you are saying." Apparently what the pastor said with his hands was not in harmony with the words coming out of his mouth.

The story made me think how easy it is for us to say one thing through our words, but something else through our behavior. The practice is common enough to have given rise to the saying, "Do as I say, not as I do." As followers of Jesus we confess that he is our Savior and Lord. We are called to match our words with behavior that gives evidence that we really believe what we say.

We are constantly confronted by temptations toward behavior which does not match our confession. The good news is that we are not abandoned to deal with such temptations by ourselves.

IN OUR SCATTERED THOUGHTS

Jesus, who was victorious when tempted, is with us to share his victory so what we say with our hands can be in harmony with our profession of faith.

Blessings as the Lord guides your mouth and hands to speak in unison.

GLIMPSES OF GOD'S PRESENCE

Strength in Weakness

My grace is sufficient for you, for my power is made perfect in weakness.

II Corinthians 12:9

"When it comes to God, I've discovered, you don't need two legs to dance." Those words came in an e-mail from a friend who had gone through four months of pain and misdiagnosis before she was finally told that she had a large tumor in her leg. At the pronouncement she closed her eyes and said, "Lord, I can't do anything about this....I can't turn back time. I can't make it go away....I can't do anything except place myself totally in your care."

She wrote, "I could have given up on life and asked to die.... But once I had left matters in God's hands, I didn't worry about it any more. I was at peace." Now, after many months of treatments, an amputation, therapy and recovery she can say, "I've chosen to look at things this way...at this point God has given me two lives...one with two legs and this current one with one leg."

This friend, like so many followers of Jesus, has experienced the grace of God in the midst of adversity, and has become stronger in her faith and more aware of the loving, caring, strengthening presence of God through it.

The Apostle Paul discovered how God can use difficult life experiences to strengthen our relationship with him. He prayed repeatedly that "a thorn in the flesh" would be taken away. God's answer: "My

160

grace is sufficient for you." This experience led Paul to write, "I will boast all the more gladly of my weakness, so that the power of Christ may dwell in me."

Blessings as you experience the grace of God in all circumstances.

God's Presence in
Grace and Forgiveness

Found

I myself will search for my sheep, and will seek them out.

Ezekiel 34:11

A sixty-five year old woman who lives in a rural area west of Spokane walked over to a neighbor's house. After an enjoyable visit, she started walking toward home, but she did not arrive at her destination because, suffering from Alzheimers disease, she became lost. Her husband reported her missing and soon sheriff's deputies and dogs were searching for her. A search and rescue helicopter with heat sensing equipment was dispatched from Fairchild Air Force Base. Shortly after midnight the helicopter crew located the woman and was able to rescue her. She would not have lived very much longer in the sub-freezing temperatures. It would be interesting to know how many person hours and how much money was expended in the search for the woman, but no one is worrying about that, because a precious life was saved.

It's a high tech version of Jesus' story about the shepherd going out to search for the lost sheep. The Old Testament is replete with references to God as a shepherd who searches for his sheep when they are lost. In the New Testament Jesus refers to himself as the Good Shepherd.

We have known it in our lives. Our forgetfulness of the Lord's goodness, and his rightful place in our lives, causes us to wander

GLIMPSES OF GOD'S PRESENCE

at times. God is like that helicopter crew, searching for us, not content to let us remain out in the cold air of doubt, despair, cynicism and forgetfulness which threatens to suck life from us. He works, at great cost, to bring us back into the safety of his presence.

Blessings as you are in that safe place.

IN GRACE AND FORGIVENESS

Case Dismissed

*Since all have sinned and fall short of the glory of
God; they are now justified by his grace as a gift,
through the redemption that is in Christ Jesus.*
Romans 3:23-24

"I've never seen that happen before," was the comment of a lawyer at the strange turn of events in a Fairfax County, VA, courtroom. A deaf couple, about to be evicted for not paying the rent, was brought to court. A change in their circumstances had unexpectedly reduced their income, and they were caught in a cash flow crunch. The judge listened to the case, then excused himself from the courtroom for a few minutes. When he came back he handed the couple two one hundred dollar bills and one fifty dollar bill. He told them to pay their rent, and dismissed the case. Something in their circumstances moved him to mercy and he paid the bill from his own funds.

The lawyer had never seen it before in the courtroom, but there is precedent for such action. We share a story where something similar happened nearly 2000 years ago on a hill outside Jerusalem. The creator and judge of this world showed mercy on his human creatures, and cancelled out the judgment against them. The price was extremely high-the death of God in the person of Jesus.

I don't know if the judge's action had a lasting effect on the deaf couple's thoughts and behavior, but I know that countless people who have received God's mercy have had their lives profoundly

167

GLIMPSES OF GOD'S PRESENCE

changed by such mercy. We are moved to gratitude, and try to express it in attitudes and behavior that reflect the mercy of God as we relate to people around us.

Blessings as you rejoice in God's mercy today.

IN GRACE AND FORGIVENESS

What Did I Do To Deserve This

Bless the Lord, O my soul, and do not forget all his benefits—who forgives all your iniquity...who crowns you with steadfast love and mercy, who satisfies you with good as long as you live.
Psalm 103:2-5

Have you ever heard someone say, "What did I do to deserve this?" Usually the question is asked when something bad has happened: an accident, illness, disappointment, or being treated unfairly. Have you ever heard the question asked when something good has happened? "What did I do to deserve such goodness?" Or do we assume that we deserve nothing but good in life?

A friend once said to me, "The person who complains he or she did not get what he (she) deserved should be thankful." That statement rose from the recognition that we are all sinners before God, and he could justly send punishment.

I am overwhelmed by a God who blesses when he could just as well punish. As persons who have received his supreme blessing in Jesus, we are called to remember his blessings, and then to thank and praise him. This is the day the Lord has given us, and again it is a day in which we can thank him for receiving what we have not deserved.

Blessings as you rejoice in God's goodness to you.

GLIMPSES OF GOD'S PRESENCE

The Evidence in the Blood

*For freedom Christ has set us free. Stand firm,
therefore, and do not submit again to a yoke of
slavery.*

Galatians 5:1

In 1983 Kenneth Waters was sent to the Walpole, MA, prison for a murder he claimed he did not commit. His sister, a high school dropout, went to college, worked her way through law school and became her brother's attorney. After the advent of DNA analysis, she hunted down the blood samples from her brother's case in a long forgotten box in the courthouse. The blood taken from the crime scene did not match Kenneth's. The prosecutors agreed that his conviction should be overturned, and he walked out of prison a free man, after 18 years of incarceration.

As I read about this case I was reminded of another event in which blood has been involved in making freedom possible. It was blood that was shed on Calvary nearly 2000 years ago. It was not that an innocent person was set free, but that countless guilty persons were set free through the death of The Innocent One. Through the mystery of God's love and grace, culminating in the death and resurrection of Jesus, we are declared "Not guilty." How this could be is far beyond my comprehension, but that does not mean it is beyond acceptance. Multitudes have experienced the joy of freedom through Jesus.

IN GRACE AND FORGIVENESS

As we experience the joy of that freedom we are powerfully motivated to use our lives constructively for the sake of others. This One who has served and saved us calls us to walk with him in the way of proclaiming liberty to the captives and freedom to the oppressed.

Blessings as you rejoice in your freedom through Jesus.

GLIMPSES OF GOD'S PRESENCE

Plea Bargaining

*There is therefore now no condemnation for those
who are in Christ Jesus.*

Romans 8:1

The newspaper carried a story about a woman charged with kid-
naping pleading guilty to lesser charges in exchange for agreeing
to be a witness against two men who were also involved in the
case. She received a greatly reduced sentence in exchange for her
testimony. The prosecutor gained something also, not having the
expense and effort of taking her case to trial, and making the trial
of the two men easier for him to win.

As I read the Scriptures, I don't find any suggestion that there will
be a possibility of any plea bargaining for us in the last judgment.
Before a holy and righteous God we all stand guilty, and he has
all the evidence necessary to convict us. The Scriptures hold out
something much better than a plea bargain in the offer of complete forgiveness through the death and resurrection of Jesus.
The Biblical story is about God who entered into our humanity
to take the full punishment of our guilt upon himself at Calvary's
cross. When we are ready to confess that we are guilty as charged,
he offers forgiveness through Jesus. Trusting that promise is the
open hand which accepts the offer.

We are overwhelmed by joy and gratitude at such a gift. Then we
discover a strange thing happening. Paul describes it as being a
slave of Jesus Christ. It is not the slavery of chains, whips, threats,

IN GRACE AND FORGIVENESS

and fear, but the slavery of love. The love of Jesus binds us to himself, and in the wonder of being loved we discover the bonds to be very freeing.

Blessings as you rejoice in the freedom/slavery which is yours in Jesus.

GLIMPSES OF GOD'S PRESENCE

Surprised By the King

For by grace you have been saved through faith,
and this is not your doing; it is the gift of God.
Ephesians 2:8

An Associated Press story told of a young man who threw a strawberry cake in the face of King Carl XVI Gustaf of Sweden. The sixteen-year-old was promptly wrestled to the ground and arrested by the police. The king then asked the young man if he was OK. I was surprised at the monarch's question. I would have expected that his status, as well as anger over getting a cake in the face, would have prompted quite a different response. He showed amazing concern for a young punk.

The story prompted me to think of God's attitude toward us. One of the titles we use for him is king, emphasizing his authority and power. Amazingly, he does not use that authority and power for self-serving ends, but wields them under the control of his grace, mercy, and concern. More than once we have thrown cake in his face as we have defied him and insisted that our way of doing things is better than his. We claim that we are created in his image, but demonstrate how distorted that image is as we refuse to follow him in the pathway of humble service and love. We soft pedal his commands, and like to think that he gave us ten suggestions. And he comes down to ask us if we are OK. Of course, not everything is OK with us, but he loves us in spite of ourselves, and has dealt with all that is wrong through hanging on a cross.

Blessings as you marvel at God's grace.

The Fresh Air of Grace

While we were still weak, at the right time Christ
died for the ungodly....God proves his love for us in
that while we still were sinners Christ died for us.
Romans 5:6, 8

I suspect that you have received numerous e-mail messages with the rquest to pass them on to a specific number of people. Often they include a promise that if you comply with the request something wonderful will happen to you. I received one of those forwarded messages which had a completely different ending: "Pass this on to someone else, if you'd like. There is NO LUCK attached. If you delete this, its okay: God's Love Is Not Dependent On E-Mail!!" It came as a refreshing breath of fresh air, having no expectation connected with it. THAT'S GRACE!

Many demands and requirements are laid upon us, both by other people and by ourselves. In school, at work, in our marriages, in family living, and in business and social relationships we are expected to behave in certain ways. What a breath of fresh air when grace breaks into this world of requirement bearing a word of forgiveness, hope and encouragement. Some people have a knack for bringing that grace into our lives. They reflect what God has done to deal with all our sin, guilt, failure, and broken relationships as he offers forgiveness and new life through a crucifixion and resurrection.

GLIMPSES OF GOD'S PRESENCE

We will always live in a world of demands and requirements. God has expectations of us as well. But the overwhelming good news of the Christian faith is that we are surrounded by God's amazing grace at the very point where we cannot fulfill the requirements.

Blessings as you breathe the fresh air of grace.

IN GRACE AND FORGIVENESS

Dealing With Imperfections

And you who once were estranged and hostile in mind, doing evil deeds, he has now reconciled in his fleshly body through death, so as to present you holy and blameless and irreproachable before him.

Colossians 1:21-22

Another task was completed in my basement finishing project. Some molding was put in place around a door, the nails were set, and holes were filled with putty. How good it is to have putty that can, at least partially, hide the holes and imperfections–particularly those corner joints which did not fit perfectly. If I were a more skilled carpenter, perhaps I would not need to fill in the joints. They were really pretty good, but the cracks did show. Thanks to putty, now they are not very obvious.

As I was working I began thinking how our lives are like the imperfect cuts and the nail holes. Through life we try to use various kinds of putty so those faults and failures will not be completely obvious to other people. We hide much of what we are from others.

We may try to hide the faults from God, too, even though we know that is a futile effort. The good news is that we do not have to cover up as far as God is concerned. He has come to us in the person of Jesus to deal with all those failings, and present us as holy,

GLIMPSES OF GOD'S PRESENCE

blameless and irreproachable. That certainly does not describe the way we live out life, but it does describe the way God considers us and treats us because of the crucifixion of Jesus. Wow! It makes me want to try to live up to that image.

Blessings on you, holy, blameless, and irreproachable one.

IN GRACE AND FORGIVENESS

The Fare Isn't Fair

The free gift is not like the effect of one man's sin.
For the judgment following one trespass brought
condemnation, but the free gift following many
trespasses brings justification.

Romans 5:16

Have you ever stopped to think while on an airplane that the person sitting next to you may have paid half as much for their ticket as you did for yours? Or twice as much? On a given flight there are many different fares. We might question whether the fares are fair.

God is like the airlines. His fare for the journey to the eternal segment of the kingdom is not fair. If it were fair, none of us could afford it. But it is a free ride for us through the grace he has demonstrated in Jesus. Costly for him (a crucifixion), but free for us.

Yet there is the paradox. When we accept it, it costs us everything. We cannot accept the gift and go our own way. We are powerfully moved to go His way. Jesus indicates it involves denying ourselves, taking up our cross and following him. As we try it out, we discover this is not a burden, but a privilege—a way of thanking him for the gift.

Blessings as you have a joy-filled flight today.

Power to Forgive

Clothe yourselves with the new self, created according to the likeness of God in true righteousness and holiness.

Ephesians 4:24

Wayne and Kathryn were new acquaintances and delightful dinner partners when Marilyn and I ate with them in the dining room at St. Mary's Lodge on the eastern edge of Glacier Park. At Kathryn's prompting Wayne, who was paralyzed from the waist down and dependent upon a wheel chair for mobility, told us about the circumstances of his injury. He came home one evening and found an intruder in his house. The young man panicked and shot Wayne, injuring his spinal cord. Wayne looked up at him and said, "You don't realize what you have just done. You have attacked a child of God. You bear a heavy burden of guilt, but I forgive you." The assailant looked down at him for a moment with wonder in his eyes, then fled.

Wow! I'm not sure I could have said something like that if I had been lying on that floor in a pool of blood. How could he do it? I think Wayne would tell us that the motivation came from outside himself. Our conversation that evening gave evidence that the wonder of God's love and forgiveness through Jesus had permeated his heart, and prompted his response to the evil inflicted upon him. It would never have happened if the foundation of his life had not been a vital relationship with Jesus. That relationship

IN GRACE AND FORGIVENESS

helped him move through recovery and rehab, to deal with all the emotions arising from being shot and robbed of his ability to walk, and gave him a wonderfully positive outlook on life.

Blessings as the transforming power of the Risen Jesus is at work in your life.

GLIMPSES OF GOD'S PRESENCE

Reconciliation at the Table

May the God of steadfastness and encouragement
grant you to live in harmony with one another, in
accordance with Jesus Christ.

Romans 15:5

Two women came from differing parts of the church and by chance knelt next to each other at the Communion rail. Some weeks earlier one of the women had spoken some harsh words to the other. As the two were kneeling, the woman of harsh words touched the arm of the other and said, "Mary, will you forgive me?" Reconciliation took place at the Lord's Table.

How many of us are carrying the memories of words we wish we had never spoken? Which one of us does not feel the pain of speech we wish we had never heard? How many of us know some of the ache in our hearts would be diminished if there could be confession and forgiveness, but somehow it never happens?

Thankfully, the two women were led by the Spirit of God to a place where it could happen. I'm sure their story could be told countless times in a variety of forms as people have been brought together in the presence of the crucified, risen, and living Jesus.

Through the death and resurrection of Jesus we have been declared to be forgiven ones. As we marvel at, and give thanks for, that gracious reconciliation, something happens in our inner being so that it becomes more possible for us to apologize to and

IN GRACE AND FORGIVENESS

seek reconciliation with others. True, reconciliation cannot happen if one person will have nothing to do with it, but we have been shown that when people meet at the foot of the cross the Spirit of God works with power.

Blessings as you are empowered to apologize and to forgive.

GLIMPSES OF GOD'S PRESENCE

The Cover-up

*I acknowledged my sin to you, and I did not hide
my iniquity; I said, "I will confess my transgressions
to the Lord," and you forgave the guilt of my sin.*
Psalm 32:5

An e-mail message to a friend to inform her that three of my devotionals had been accepted for publication in a well known magazine which is published in several languages elicited this response: "Just think! You will be talking to 5,000,000 PEOPLE with each of your deviations."

I think she intended to write, "devotions." At least I hope so. I certainly do not want my deviations so widely published. I am much more comfortable in the cover-up society of Adam and Eve, than in having my sin exposed for all the world to see. At the same time, I deplore the cover-up attempts of prominent political figures, business executives, and others. How much better it would be for everyone if they would forthrightly confess their faults. To avoid hypocrisy, I have to admit that it is better if I do the same.

God calls us to confess our sin to him, not simply as an exercise in exposure, but as a step toward receiving forgiveness and healing. Isaiah celebrates the way God deals with our sins as he writes, "I will greatly rejoice in the Lord, my whole being shall exult in my God; for he has clothed me with the garments of salvation, he has covered me with the robe of righteousness" (Isaiah 61:10).

184

IN GRACE AND FORGIVENESS

The New Testament proclamation is that he does it through the death and resurrection of Jesus. Now, that is the kind of cover-up I need.

Blessings as you confess and God's covers.

Forgiveness Is a Decision

Bear with one another and, if anyone has a complaint against another, forgive each other.

Colossians 3:13

Marilyn showed me a quote from Charles Dickens: "May I tell you why it seems to me a good thing to remember wrong that has been done to us? That we may forgive it."

Oh, that Dickens might speak to us today! We live in an unforgiving culture which expresses itself in road rage, shootings, abuse (verbal and physical), and a variety of other actions. All of us have been wronged (and, yes, we have wronged others). All of us have the opportunity to extend the grace of forgiveness. A note of caution, though, as we talk about forgiveness: it is different from overlooking and putting up with the actions of abusive people.

There have been times when it has been difficult to have any positive feelings toward a person who has wronged me. As I have struggled with this, I have realized that forgiveness isn't as much about feelings (which we cannot control) as it is about decisions and actions (which we can control). There are at least four decisions involved in forgiveness:

1. I will not take revenge on the person.

2. I will pray for the person who wronged me.

3. I will do good for the person if he or she needs my help.

4. I will pray that more positive feelings will follow.

IN GRACE AND FORGIVENESS

We, and society, are blessed as we become more forgiving persons. The power to become that kind of person lies in marveling at God's forgiveness of us through Jesus, and thanking him for it.

Blessings as you make decisions to forgive.

GLIMPSES OF GOD'S PRESENCE

Accomplished: Mission Impossible

Come now, let us argue it out, says the Lord: though your sins are like scarlet, they shall be like snow; though they are red like crimson, they shall become like wool.

Isaiah 1:18

Have you ever heard of the tolaath worm? That is the Hebrew name for what is scientifically named coccus ilicis. If a poll were to be conducted of all who will be reading this, I suspect that we would conclude that the tolaath worm does not have a very good press agent. The worm was used in biblical times for making a very expensive crimson dye which did not fade with washing or exposure to sunlight, and was impossible to bleach out–very unusual characteristics for dyes of that day.

The Scriptures tell us that all have sinned and fallen short of the glory of God. Some of us may have committed very grievous sins. Many of us probably have not–at least not those which are considered utterly terrible by contemporary human standards. But whatever our sin, the guilt of it is like the crimson die of the tolaath worm. There is no way we can remove it. But the promise of God through the prophet Isaiah and the Savior Jesus is that God does the impossible through a crucifixion and a resurrection. Through Jesus the crimson disappears and we are clothed in the white robes of righteousness to be presented as holy, blameless and irreproachable (Colossians 1:22). Isn't that good news! We don't have to accept the wonderful gift, but God certainly invites us to.

Blessings as you rejoice in God doing the impossible with you.

IN GRACE AND FORGIVENESS

A Trip to the Dump

*God proves his love for us in that while we still were
sinners Christ died for us.*
Romans 5:8

At the memorial service for Pastor Carl a family member recounted how, back in the years before Waste Management and waste transfer stations, he made frequent trips to the dump to discard garbage and items that he considered no longer useful. But he always came back from the dump with something someone else had thrown away. He was sure he could restore it and make it useful again. He had a way of seeing value where others may see only trash, including pieces of driftwood and old boards which he creatively transformed into items of interest.

We reflected on how his going to the dump mirrored the Gospel this elderly and beloved former pastor proclaimed. God sees humanity, broken and deserving to be discarded because of our sin and rebellion against our Creator. But God still values and loves his creatures and wants to restore us to fellowship with him and shape us for life in his kingdom. The history-changing life, death, and resurrection of Jesus is his way of reclaiming us and bringing us back.

Countless individuals through the centuries have given evidence of the power of Jesus to bring them back, to shape their lives, and to make them a blessing to those around them. Many of us realize that we need to be brought back repeatedly.

Blessings as Jesus reclaims and restores you.

God's Presence in
Faith, Hope, and Love

IN FAITH, HOPE, AND LOVE

Faith: Strong and Fragile

So if you think you are standing, watch out that you do not fall.
I Corinthians 10:12

Has someone commented to you about your strong faith? Has someone seen you as an example of what it means to live by faith? If so, I rejoice with you. Have you thought of yourself as a person of strong faith? If so, beware.

Faith can be tremendously strong, but also surprisingly fragile. Faith inspired the disciples of Jesus, withstanding fierce opposition, to proclaim him as the crucified and risen Savior. The miracle of the Church rose from their faithful preaching. The power of faith made Paul the great missionary who endured imprisonment, stonings, beatings, and shipwreck in his endeavor to spread the good news of Jesus. Martin Luther, inspired by faith, stood firm against the pope and the emperor to lead the Reformation and change the face of western civilization. You can think of people you know who, through faith, have had an impact on life around them. Faith is powerful.

Faith is fragile. It is like humility in that as soon as we start boasting about it we are in danger of losing genuine faith. We remember that Peter boasted that he would never deny Jesus, but soon afterward was telling the servant girl that he did not know Jesus. Faith is not something we create, but is God's gift to us–a gift which is renewed day by day. One shot of faith will not keep us

193

GLIMPSES OF GOD'S PRESENCE

for a lifetime. Christian faith is an intimate trust relationship with God. Like human relationships, if it is not nurtured it languishes. Faith is fragile.

Blessings as you rejoice in the gift of faith which God strengthens in you today.

IN FAITH, HOPE, AND LOVE

Trusting the Father

*God is our refuge and strength, a very present help
in trouble.*

Psalm 46:1

With its mountains and fjords, Norway has some spectacular
scenery. Frequently one can see small farms clinging to the gentler slopes of those rugged mountains. When a cousin came from
Norway to visit us, she shared a story about a man who had grown
up on one of those farms. When he was about 10 years old, a lamb
fell off a cliff which dropped down toward the fjord far below. Fortunately the lamb landed on a small ledge a few feet below the
edge of the cliff, but there was no way a person could climb down
to rescue it. The farmer tied a rope around his young son, and lowered him down to the ledge. The boy untied the rope from himself
and tied it to the lamb so his father could raise it to safety. Then
the rope was lowered again so the boy could be raised.

The person who was interviewing the boy, now grown to be an
older man, asked, "Weren't you terribly afraid dangling there between the sky and the sea?" The man answered, "No, I was not
afraid because my father was holding the rope."

Have you sometimes felt like you were dangling between the sky
and the sea? Life brings us times of uncertainty; precarious, stressful, frightening times. In those times we can be assured that our
Father is holding the rope.

Blessings as you are held by God's strong hands.

GLIMPSES OF GOD'S PRESENCE

Faith Catches Us

*Faith comes from what is heard, and what is heard
comes through the word of Christ.*

Romans 10:17

Eric was feeling very discouraged when he came to his pastor. He had run up against some problems at work and at home which had been emotionally draining. He was beginning to feel that God had abandoned him. When asked what he wanted most, he did not hesitate in replying, "I want my faith back. Where has it gone? How can I get it again?"

How can we get faith for the tough days of life? Sometimes it may seem like a butterfly, fluttering hither and yon on a sunny day, but not to be found when it rains. Sometimes it may seem like a super ball, bouncing unpredictably off hard surfaces, and almost impossible to catch. We try to get control of faith, but discover we can't.

Faith comes quietly, and catches us. It is the gift of God. The Holy Spirit bestows faith, using Word and Sacraments as his means. What we can do is put ourselves in the places where we can hear, and faith can catch us. Faith is not something we can suddenly call up for a crisis if it has not been nurtured beforehand. Hearing, reading, and pondering the promises of the Word in the quiet moments will nurture the faith which can stand up in the crisis. I thank God for the gift of faith: faith which centers in Jesus who hung on the cross; faith which, seeing Jesus, knows God's presence in the tough times of life.

Blessings as you let the Spirit build faith in you today.

IN FAITH, HOPE, AND LOVE

Untroubled Hearts

*Do not let your hearts be troubled. Believe in God,
believe also in me.*

John 14:1

Circumstances would tell us that it must have been a troubling time for Jesus on the evening before his crucifixion. As he gave bread and wine to his disciples he spoke the words, "My body given for you....My blood shed for you." He had told them that one of them would betray him, and another deny him. And yet he said, "Let not your hearts be troubled," and gave them the promise of a place in the Father's house. I marvel that he could be so concerned for others in such an hour. What is his secret?

The secret of untroubled hearts lies in his words, "Believe in God, believe also in me."

Through many years of pastoral ministry I have been privileged to see some followers of Jesus go through severe storms in their lives with great calmness. They would speak of knowing they are held in the arms of a loving Father. They believe (trust) in God who has made himself known to us in Jesus. I am thankful for these witnesses to the validity of Jesus' promises.

If you are going through stress-filled days right now, may you hear again the words of Jesus for you: "Let not your hearts be troubled; believe in God, believe also in me."

Peace to you as you listen to these words of Jesus .

GLIMPSES OF GOD'S PRESENCE

The Pilot

For we walk by faith, not by sight.
II Corinthians 5:7

Occasionally Marilyn and I board an airplane to fly to wherever our daughter and her Air Force husband, and our two delightful granddaughters are stationed. As we travel we entrust our lives to some pilots. That is a type of living by faith. I am glad they do not point to me as I board the plane and say, "It is your turn to be pilot today." What a disaster that would be.

In our spiritual lives we are called to do something similar–entrust our lives to Jesus. Too often I find that I want to take control of that flight–to go in my preferred direction on my time schedule. Sometimes I think my plans and goals are more pleasant than the direction he seems to be taking me. Is that true for you as well? In our best moments we realize that safety and well being depends upon him being in control. He knows the destination and best route much better than we do, having been there before us, and is in better communication with the control tower. Our job is not to fly the plane, but to be responsible crew members, caring for others on the journey.

Blessings on your journey today as you travel with faith in Jesus.

IN FAITH, HOPE, AND LOVE

Hope for the Future

*Seek the Lord and his strength, seek his presence
continually. Remember the wonderful works he
has done, his miracles, and the judgments he
uttered.*

I Chronicles 16:11-12

It was a glorious October day in Spokane! The sun was shining
brilliantly in a beautiful blue sky marked by the contrails of some
airplanes. The evidence of God's paint brush was in the reds and
golds of the trees. The Spokane River sparkled and foamed as the
strong current moved over and around the rocks in the river bed.
It was the kind of day that inspires a person to pause and thank
God for the beauty of the earth, and the sky, and the water. Yes,
God is good, and he loves beauty.

I hope I can remember and revel in the beauty of this day
when some of the dreary and drippy days, or the windy and
biting cold days come later in the year. In recalling the delightful weather I can live in hope that there will again be pleasant
days.

In our emotional and spiritual lives there are sometimes stormy,
miserable, trying, painful days. Then, too, it is good to draw on our
memory of what God has provided in the past to give us hope for
the future. We remember the story of how he has acted to bring
the sunshine of his saving love into this world. We remember his
promises through Jesus that he will be with us always, and that

199

GLIMPSES OF GOD'S PRESENCE

there is nothing in all creation which can separate us from his love. Remembering, we have hope for God's loving, caring, uplifting, and encouraging presence in the todays and the tomorrows of life.

Blessings as you build those memories.

IN FAITH, HOPE, AND LOVE

Living Forever

And this is what he has promised us, eternal life.
I John 2:25

In a conversation with Marilyn a woman commented, "Your mother is 105. You are going to live forever." Knowing the woman's solid Christian faith, Marilyn replied, "Yes, and so are you."

Because of the hope that is ours through the crucifixion and resurrection of Jesus, we can look with joyful anticipation beyond our days on this earth with confidence that eternity will be spent in the loving presence of our Lord. That hope does not diminish the significance of life on earth, but gives it fuller meaning as preparation for life in that other segment of God's kingdom.

We don't have many clues about what that life will be like. I doubt that we will spend all our time sitting around listening to music and playing harps. If our inclinations are toward athletics rather than toward music, that would not be a very exciting prospect. Since life on earth is enriched by having meaningful responsibilities, I suspect there will be a variety of meaningful responsibilities in the after life. Of this I am sure: we will enjoy the fullness of God's presence in a way we cannot imagine now. Another certainty for me is that we are all in for a big surprise, and it will be good.

In the meantime, Jesus tells us that those who believe in him have eternal life right now (John 6:47). It is not fully realized yet, but we

201

GLIMPSES OF GOD'S PRESENCE

are experiencing a foretaste as we live as followers of Jesus. What we have known of that relationship is good, and we look forward to more.

Blessings as you live the life which is eternal today.

IN FAITH, HOPE, AND LOVE

The Best Part of the Day

We wait for the blessed hope and the manifestation of the glory of our great God and Savior, Jesus Christ.

Titus 2:13

When our children were small Marilyn and I established a bedtime tradition of asking, "What was the best part of your day?" When we asked that question one December 24, our daughter answered without hesitation, "Having Christmas tomorrow." The sense of anticipation had given color and joy to her whole day in a wonderful way.

Life can become very dull and drab if we are living without a sense of anticipation. If we are caught in the doldrums of days without meaning, and the days to come seem to hold only more of the same, there is not much reason for joy. But if we can live in the spirit that "Christmas is coming tomorrow," this day can be wonderful.

As followers of Jesus we have reason to live with a sense of anticipation. For today there is the promise that the risen Lord is with his people. Where will he lead us today? What opportunities for service will he set before us? How will he demonstrate his encouragement and protection? In what way will he prompt our growth in faith?

There is anticipation for the future as we hear the promise, "In my Father's house there are many dwelling places....I will come again and take you to myself, so that where I am, there you may be also" (John 14:2-3). If that is not something to brighten this day, I don't know what will.

Blessings as you live in anticipation.

GLIMPSES OF GOD'S PRESENCE

Death, Comfort and Hope

"Death has been swallowed up in victory"....Thanks be to God, who gives us the victory through our Lord Jesus Christ.

I Corinthians 15:54, 57

There was a cloud over the beautiful, clear, crisp day as we would be attending the funeral of a dear friend. She had gone in for knee surgery, and was apparently doing well. About a week after her surgery, her husband and her daughter were with her about supper time and she told them to go out and get something to eat, because she was doing fine. When they stopped briefly in the visitors' room, they heard monitor alarms going off and saw people rushing into her room. She had died of cardiac arrest.

Trying to share comfort, we feel our words are so inadequate. In God's Word we find hope. Because of Jesus' resurrection we are promised that death is not the end of the journey for us. "If we live, we live to the Lord, and if we die, we die to the Lord; so then, whether we live or whether we die, we are the Lord's" (Romans 14:8).

These are words of comfort and hope as we are confronted with the death of loved ones. They are also words for us as we consider our own mortality. The unknown about death can cause fear. But there is the known: We belong to the Lord....We are in his hands.... He is with us....The resurrection lies ahead. Therefore, we can walk this day in confidence, living thankfully for what God has done for us in Jesus, relying on the powerful name of Jesus.

Blessings in your joys and sorrows.

IN FAITH, HOPE, AND LOVE

Breaking Through the Clouds

For once you were darkness, but now in the Lord you are light. Live as children of light–for the fruit of the light is found in all that is good and right and true.

Ephesians 5:8-9

Rain drizzled from the dark grey clouds as we boarded the airplane. While taxiing toward the runway, we saw puddles of water in every low spot. We expected the rain to continue falling for the entire day. The accelerating airplane pushed us back into our seats, and soon we began climbing in a steep ascent. Suddenly we broke through the cloud cover and found ourselves in brilliant sunshine.

"What a parable for life," I thought. A dark cloud cover often hangs over our lives. Disappointments, sorrow, grief, temptations, and failure strip the brightness from us. The news of terrorist attacks, corporate greed, unethical behavior adds to our discouragement. We begin to suspect that the rain is going to fall continually.

Many of us, through the miracle of God's grace, have been lifted above the clouds to see the brightness of God's love in Jesus. The Kingdom of Heaven has broken in on us, and the Spirit of God has shown us that there is more than life beneath the clouds. The good news in Jesus announces forgiveness, abundant life, mercy, healing, comfort, and hope.

GLIMPSES OF GOD'S PRESENCE

Our lives cannot always be above the pain and discouragement which surround us. But we, who have seen the wonder of God's grace in Jesus, know that the Son is beyond the clouds and he holds us in his love.

Blessings as God lifts you to see the light of his grace.

IN FAITH, HOPE, AND LOVE

Constant Grace

The Lord is good; his steadfast love endures forever.

Psalm 100:5

A newspaper carried a 1928 picture of a crowded grandstand at a local race track. Almost all the men were dressed in suits, ties, and hats. Several young boys wore suits, ties, and caps. The women were attired in dresses and high-heeled shoes. I wonder if there is a race track in the world today where you could find people so dressed up. Or for that matter, is there a church? Changing fashions reflect life around us, which is changing at an astounding pace. Communications, transportation, moral standards, foods, living arrangements, worship patterns, and almost everything else is much different from just a few years ago.

In the face of all this change we read, "Jesus Christ is the same yesterday and today and forever" (Hebrews 13:8). Does that mean that Jesus is out of touch with the times, and should be discarded along with those 1928 clothes? Hardly! It means that the grace and love of God revealed in Jesus is constant and fits every age of human history. Whether we ride in a horse-drawn buggy or a jet airplane, we need God's love, acceptance, and forgiveness as much now as humans have ever needed it. Jesus is the constant evidence that the faithfulness of God can be counted on when we can depend on nothing else. The power of that event at the cross,

207

GLIMPSES OF GOD'S PRESENCE

which stands at the intersection of human history, comes through the ages to claim us as reconciled and forgiven children of God. Jesus is still the one who can bring hope, peace, and joy in the midst of our tumultuous times.

Blessings as you rely on that constant grace of God.

IN FAITH, HOPE, AND LOVE

She Knew Her Sheep

I am the good shepherd. I know my own and my own know me, just as the Father knows me and I know the Father. And I lay down my life for the sheep.

John 10:14-15

One day when I was a pastor in Ritzville, WA I drove out to visit one of our farm families. Entering the driveway, I saw a young girl of the family near an enclosure in which there were five sheep. "Pastor, these are my sheep for a 4-H project," she commented as she proceeded to tell me the name of each one. They all looked alike to me, and since they would not stand still, it was not long before I had no idea which was which. But she knew. She also began telling me about their characteristics: "This one closest to us is aggressive. The one in that corner is quite submissive. The one by the fence is stubborn." They were her sheep, and she cared for them, cared about them, and knew them.

I am reminded of that girl every time I read the words of Jesus about being the Good Shepherd who knows his sheep. We are not numbers in some heavenly computer. As people who are drawn by the Spirit of God to know, trust, love, and follow Jesus, we are known by him. He knows our names, our characteristics, our strengths, our weaknesses, our victories, our defeats, our joys, our sorrows. It is a knowing which flows out of his love–love so

GLIMPSES OF GOD'S PRESENCE

great that he laid down his life for us. What comfort and encouragement that brings as we move through life!

Blessings as you live this day in the wonder being known and loved by your Lord.

IN FAITH, HOPE, AND LOVE

The Sign of Life

*You show me the path of life. In your presence there
is fullness of joy; in your right hand are pleasures
forevermore.*

Psalm 16:11

The early signs of fall were visible as Marilyn and I took our morning walk. Most noticeable were the bushes on the hillside which had exchanged the green in their leaves for a dark reddish brown. The tall grasses along the way were golden and heavily laden with seeds. The alfalfa field had received its last cutting of the season and the bales had been hauled away. The dark brown cattails stood erect and many of the leaves on the tomato plants had dried up and fallen off, exposing the ripening fruit.

I began to reflect that life is turning toward fall for the two of us. While we have been blessed with excellent health, we have discovered that we move a bit more slowly, we don't have the energy we used to, and there is an occasional touch of arthritis. They are just little signs at this point that the winter of life is approaching.

But something else was evident during our walk: the predominant color on the hillside was not that reddish brown, but the deep, vibrant green of the pine trees. They will keep that color through the winter and into next spring and summer. They were a reminder that the color of life is predominant for us as well. Jesus

211

GLIMPSES OF GOD'S PRESENCE

destroyed the power of death through the cross and his glorious resurrection. Through the power of that resurrection he draws his followers into the life which death cannot overcome. We live with the confident hope that life, not death, rules our future.

Blessings as life receives its eternal hue through Jesus.

IN FAITH, HOPE, AND LOVE

Encouragers

*Encourage one another and build up each other....
encourage the fainthearted, help the weak, be
patient with all of them.*

I Thess. 5:11, 14

It was a delightful experience to watch our granddaughters participate in their events and to observe the crowd as Marilyn and I attended a Montana State swim meet. I was impressed by how encouraging and supportive the crowd was of the swimmers. I did not hear a discouraging or critical word all day. One event in particular caught my attention. A seven-year-old boy had almost 25 meters left in the 50 meter free style race when the others had already finished. All eyes were on the boy as he struggled toward the end of the pool. When he finally touched the timing device, the crowd joined in a loud cheer and in the clapping of hands. You would have thought he had won the most important race of the day.

Don't you wish the world outside the swimming arena would exhibit that same kind of spirit? So often we are confronted by criticism and confrontation. The Church does not seem to be immune from discouraging spirits. As followers of Jesus we are called to a different path–that of encouraging and building up each other.

Jesus lays the groundwork for that kind of spirit in his words, "I give you a new commandment, that you love one another. Just as I have loved you, you also should love one another" (John 13:34). As we are overcome by his tremendous love, a new spirit grows within us, and we learn to be encouragers.

Blessings as you find opportunities to give encouragement.

213

GLIMPSES OF GOD'S PRESENCE

Words of Concern

The Lord is faithful in all his words, and gracious in all his deeds.

Psalm 145:13

"You aren't going to drive back to Spokane tonight, are you?" "No, Mother. I'm going to let an airplane take me." "Oh, good!"

That was the last conversation I had with my mother, just 43 hours before her death. During the hours I had spent with her that day she spoke almost no words, as her frail 97-year-old body could do no more than produce an occasional faint whisper. But just as daylight was turning to dusk, the question came out loud and clear. A mother's concern about her son driving 300 miles during the night produced one last bit of energy and the last question of her life.

She wasn't intentionally imitating Jesus as he spoke his dying words, but perhaps it would be natural for this life-long follower of Jesus to echo her Savior's concern expressed in his last words as he said: "Father, forgive them, for they know not what they do," "...today you will be with me in Paradise," "Woman, behold, your son!...Behold, your mother!"

Those dying words of my mother were a gift to me as they underscored the love and care expressed throughout her life for me and my siblings. The dying words of Jesus are a gift to all of us. They were spoken to and about specific people around him at the time of his crucifixion, but they underline the love and concern he has for all of us as he accepted that place on the cross in our behalf.

Blessings as you are carried in the love of Jesus.

IN FAITH, HOPE, AND LOVE

Coming In Out of the Cold

Knowledge puffs up, but love builds up.
I Corinthians 8:1

The lone Ingrid Bergman rose bud's attempt to open had been thwarted by the cold weather of the last two weeks of October. The bud was so tight the deer had not even shown interest in it as they stripped the leaves from the long stem. Even though I had lost hope that we would witness any beauty in that rose, I did cut it and bring it into the house. Marilyn placed it in a vase and within a day it became a beautiful dark red flower. Marilyn commented, "All it needed was a little warmth. That's what all of us need to bloom."

As I reflect on my life, I thank God for those people who have provided the love and warmth which has enabled me to bloom: parents who cared for me and about me; relatives, teachers and friends who encouraged me; a gracious wife who has supported me. If I had grown up in a colder emotional environment I could very well have remained like that hard, tightly closed bud.

We who have experienced the warmth of God's grace and love through Jesus can rejoice as the Holy Spirit is opening up our lives as he creates the fruits of faith in us. Those fruits can enable us to reach out to people who are living in the cold and harsh world where God is ignored or shut out, seeking to draw them into his presence where they can bloom as God created them to.

Blessings as you bloom in the warmth of God's love.

GLIMPSES OF GOD'S PRESENCE

The Journey

*For I am convinced that neither death, nor life...nor
things present, nor things to come...nor anything
else in all creation, will be able to separate us from
the love of God in Christ Jesus our Lord.*

Romans 8:38, 39.

"You have a baby sister!" Eight-year-old Marilyn heard those
happy words one September evening many years ago from
some friends of her parents with whom she and her mother
had been staying for several days prior to the birth of her sister. Early the next morning those friends bundled up Marilyn
and her clothes (not in one bundle), took her to the train sta-
tion, and placed her on the train for the 400 mile trip from Spokane to Shelby, Montana. No one had explained anything to her
except that her mother and the baby were in the hospital. She
was on her first trip alone in a train car full of strangers. She re-
members being very apprehensive, and very cold. The only comforting thought stemmed from the fact that she was told that
her father would be waiting for her when the train arrived in
Shelby.

Marilyn's experience parallels ours as we travel the train of life. No
one has ever told us what lies ahead along the tracks. We don't
know whether the ride will be long or short, or whether it will
be accompanied by joy or sorrow, pain or pleasure, success or
failure.

Jesus has given us the promise that our Father will be there to

IN FAITH, HOPE, AND LOVE

meet us at the end of the journey. As his followers we may be apprehensive about some aspects of the trip, but we travel with faith and hope because we have learned to trust him.

Blessings in your journey.

God's Presence in

Special Days

IN SPECIAL DAYS

New Year's Day

This is the day the Lord has made; let us rejoice and be glad in it.

Psalm 118:24

There has been much controversy as to when the third millennium began. Was it January 1, 2000, or January 1, 2001? For the purists among us it was 2001. When the first millennium started, the calender we now use did not even exist. More than 500 years into the first millennium a monk by the name of Dionysius Exiguus attempted to calculate backwards to the birth of Christ, and the beginning of that first millennium. But most scholars now agree that he was wrong in his calculations, so that the birth of Jesus took place sometime between 6 BC and 4 BC according to our calender. So we should have celebrated the beginning of the third millennium somewhere between 1994 and 1996. Exactly when, only God knows. And that is good enough for me.

However we configure our calender, God is the creator and giver of time. This day, this year, this century, are all his gift to us. One of the strong affirmations of the Christian faith is that God not only gives time, but he is active in time. The whole biblical story is about God continually intersecting human time to work his good purposes. In the Christmas season we have a powerful reminder of that. God is still involved with our time: giving us the gift of life, preserving that life, surrounding us with a multitude of blessings, and seeking to engage us through faith in a relationship with him. He comes to meet us in the fullness of our time to bring his gift of salvation and life through Jesus.

Blessings on this day of the Lord.

GLIMPSES OF GOD'S PRESENCE

Epiphany (January 6)

*God's love was revealed among us in this way: God
sent his only Son into the world so that we might
live through him.*

I John 4:9

Epiphany. The Greek word refers to an appearance, a manifestation, and particularly a manifestation of the Divine. The Epiphany season of the Church year begins on January 6 and lasts until Ash Wednesday. With a focus on catching glimpses of who Jesus is as the Son of God, Epiphany stories include the visit of the wise men, the baptism of Jesus, and the miracle of changing water into wine—certainly glimpses of his glory.

While God's revelation of himself happened most explicitly in Jesus, God continues to approach us today to make himself known to us. We are surrounded by an environment which seems to do all it can to exclude the manifestations of the Divine from our experience. There are loud, competing voices which clamor for our attention, drowning out the voice of God. There are the busy activities of daily living which leave little time for experiencing the Divine.

Much of what happens to us in life depends upon where we put ourselves. If we want to catch glimpses of God's presence, love, and grace in our daily lives, we will put ourselves in situations where that is most likely to happen. Sometimes we can make use of such routine events as putting the key into the ignition switch as a reminder for a brief moment of prayer. And of course, making some time to prayerfully read our Bibles is an invitation to let God speak to us with his loving, quiet, yet powerful voice.

Blessings as God seeks to manifest himself to you today.

IN SPECIAL DAYS

Martin Luther King Day

*There is no longer Jew or Greek (Gentile), there is
no longer slave or free, there is no longer male and
female; for all of you are one in Christ Jesus.*
Galatians 3:28

"I have a dream!" Those famous words from Dr. Martin Luther King, Jr.
are in the thoughts of many people today as we observe his birthday.
Many of us are grateful for his work as our country has moved toward
racial equality. We have not yet progressed beyond all racial barriers,
but there certainly has been significant movement in recent years.

"I have a dream." Paul did not use those words, but he did hold
forth the vision of the abolition of racial, status, and gender barriers as he proclaimed the good news of Jesus through the verse
printed above. The Jew and Gentile divide of Paul's day was as
huge as any racial divisions today.

Paul did more than indicate that some day we would all be one in
Christ–it is already an accomplished fact. Unfortunately, we have
not done a very good job of living out that fact. But if you are united
with Jesus, you are united with every other person who is united with
Jesus, no matter how much they may differ from you. The closer we are
drawn to Jesus, the closer we are drawn to those who are his people.

God must have a great imagination as he created so much diver-
sity in this world. I am grateful he also provided a way for unity
through Jesus. My dream is that we may grow in our ability to
appreciate and enjoy that unity.

Blessings as you celebrate the unity which is in Jesus.

GLIMPSES OF GOD'S PRESENCE

Presidents Day

I urge that supplications, prayers, intercessions, and thanksgivings be made for everyone, for kings and all who are in high positions, so that we may lead a quiet and peaceable life in all godliness and dignity.

I Timothy 2:1-2

I can remember as a child observing Abraham Lincoln's birthday on February 12 and George Washington's on February 22. As school children we were happy to celebrate the greatness of those two United States presidents by not going to school. In 1968 Congress designated the third Monday in February as Washington's Birthday. Through the years the day has unofficially become a day to honor all our presidents. It is good to honor presidents (and other leaders) who have made outstanding contributions to the common good. But the day also invites us to give thanks to God for good political leaders and for the abilities and spirit he has given them.

This day also reminds me to thank God for his gift of government. Paul reminds us that "there is no authority except from God, and those authorities that exist have been instituted by God" (Romans 13:1). History has recorded the names of many officials who have abused their power. The abuses should not obscure the fact that, through the creative plan of God, authority has been given to preserve us from chaos.

IN SPECIAL DAYS

As followers of Jesus we have the responsibility of praying for our presidents and other leaders. The power inherent in their positions can be intoxicating, enticing them to forget that the office is to be used for public good rather than private gain. Our leaders need our prayers for wisdom, integrity, and the guidance of the Spirit of God.

Blessings as you pray for our leaders.

GLIMPSES OF GOD'S PRESENCE

Ash Wednesday

Humble yourselves therefore under the mighty hand of God, so that he may exalt you in due time.
I Peter 5:6

A strong westerly wind, gusting up to 50 miles per hour, swept across the farmlands and filled the air with dust. The view of the mountains to the east was obscured, and the dust was still heavy in the air as we went to the Ash Wednesday service. As we knelt at the altar, the ashes from last year's Passion Sunday palms was smudged on our foreheads, and we heard the words, "Remember, you are dust, and to dust you will return."

Me? Dust? Like the dust that filled the air? Is that all we are? The statement forced me to think out into the future and realize that, barring the Lord's early return, that's all we will be someday. For most of us, with the passing of the years, no one will remember we ever existed. If Lent is to nudge us toward humility, the ashes on our foreheads, and those words, should provide a good start.

But then I began to reflect on the biblical story, and it struck me that God must like dust. Genesis tells us that God formed humans from dust. His creative power transformed the dust into persons whom God loves and cares about. The story goes on to speak about love so great that he became dust in Jesus, whose resurrection holds the promise that returning to dust need not be the end of the story for us. Though we may soon be forgotten by future

IN SPECIAL DAYS

generations, God has promised that he will never forget us. His desire is for us to live in his home forever.

Blessings as you live as holy dust.

GLIMPSES OF GOD'S PRESENCE

Saint Patrick's Day (March 17)

*Love your enemies and pray for those who
persecute you.*

Matthew 5:44

Patrick was born to a wealthy family in England at the end of the
fourth century. When he was 16 years old, he was kidnaped by pi-
rates and sold to a Druid chieftan in Ireland where he was assigned
to care for the sheep. While out in the fields he had much time to
ponder the many Bible verses his father had taught him, and in his
"Confessions" he wrote, "At 16...in a strange land the Lord opened my
unbelieving eyes and I was converted." After six years he escaped, returned to England, and then went to France to prepare himself for
mission work in Ireland. At his request he was sent back to Ireland
and is credited with bringing Christianity to that country as he established 300 churches and baptized more than 120,000 persons.

There are legends of snakes and shamrocks surrounding this man,
but the significant thing about him is that he developed such a
love for those who enslaved him that he had a passion for sharing
the good news about Jesus with them. That is the power of the
Gospel. It is the kind of story repeated many times in the history
of the church. Love has replaced resentment.

There is reason for us to celebrate the grace of God in Patrick's life.
That example of grace can encourage us to let the Holy Spirit repeat
in us the same kind of miracle of concern and love for those toward
whom we might have reason to feel resentment and anger.

Blessings as you remember God's grace through Patrick today.

IN SPECIAL DAYS

Maundy Thursday

I give you a new commandment, that you love one another. Just as I have loved you, you also should love one another. By this everyone will know that you are my disciples, if you have love for one another.

John 13:34, 35

The Latin word for "commandment" is "mandatum." You recognize the English word "mandate" flowing from that. It is because of that mandate that we call the day before Good Friday "Maundy Thursday."

There has been much controversy, and even court cases, about the display of the ten commandments. Perhaps too much has been made of the ten commandments and too little emphasis placed upon the one commandment. Jesus does not say that he is giving us an additional commandment, but a new one. It supercedes the ten. In response to the amazing love of God, followers of Jesus are called to obey one commandment. There is no option: love one another as Jesus has loved us. If we obey that one, we will keep the others as well.

We protest, "I just cannot have loving feelings toward some people I know." The command is not to have warm feelings, but to love. Love is a decision: to treat others kindly, to encourage and build up others, to speak well of others, to help others (even our enemies) when they are in need, and to act toward others as you think Jesus would act toward them.

GLIMPSES OF GOD'S PRESENCE

We are called to walk close to Jesus, experiencing his love for us. Close to him–that's where we will receive power to love as he loves. And then the world will be blessed.

Blessings as together, in Jesus' presence, we learn love.

IN SPECIAL DAYS

Good Friday

We know that all things work together for good for
those who love God.

Romans 8:28

What's good about Good Friday? What a strange name for a day
of crucifixion.

God has a way of working in the midst of evil circumstances to
bring good out of them. This was certainly true in the crucifixion
as human anger and hatred nailed Jesus to the cross. But God
used the most tragic event in human history to bring forgiveness,
salvation and life to us. This day became in a unique way "God's
Friday."

Contemplating the events of this day we are saddened, and we
realize that the day calls for our crucifixion. All the pride, self-
centeredness, and self-righteousness which we cherish needs to
be nailed to the cross. Looking at the Son of God dying on that
cross is a humbling experience We would like to put the blame
on first century Jews and Romans, but it won't stick there. The
cross calls us to admit that our daily disregard for God's place
in our lives, our disobedience, and our giving priority to our
wishes rather than his good and gracious will, helped drive those
nails.

We hear the Dying One speak from the cross: "Father, forgive them,
for they know not what they do," and, "Today you will be with me
in paradise." Can we believe that his dying means forgiveness and
paradise for us also? Faith says, "Yes." God made this culmination

231

GLIMPSES OF GOD'S PRESENCE

of evil the instrument of his grace to deliver us from sin and death, and to offer us forgiveness and life. He turned Black Friday into Good Friday. Thanks be to God!

Blessings as this day drives you to your knees, and lifts you up in hope!

IN SPECIAL DAYS

Easter

If Christ has not been raised, then our proclamation
has been in vain and your faith has been in vain....
But in fact Christ has been raised from the dead.
I Corinthians 15:14, 20

Christ is risen!   He is risen indeed!

We joyfully join in the traditional Easter greeting as we celebrate this wonderful day. Easter is the highlight of the Christian year as we rejoice in the victory of Jesus over death. This is not merely the victory of a lone prisoner of death escaping the dungeon. It is his breaking down of the prison walls so that death cannot hold any of us captive.

When I was a pastor in Ritzville, WA, a drug store owner told me that one night someone discovered the back door of his store was improperly installed, so that the hinges were on the outside. Since this seemed to provide easy access to the store, the person removed the pins from the hinges. However, the door was wedged so tightly into the frame that it could not be removed. The next morning the owner came to unlock the door and started to open it. Naturally, the door could not swing on the hinges without the pins being in place, so it fell on him.

I see the resurrection of Jesus as the great hinge of the Christian faith. Without that resurrection Christianity does not work. The resurrection is the event which validates all that Jesus said, claimed, and did. This is indeed the pivotal event of our faith. It is the living Christ who has inspired, motivated, and empowered his

233

GLIMPSES OF GOD'S PRESENCE

people through the centuries and who invites us into the life we call eternal.

Blessings as you rejoice in Jesus' resurrection and the promise of your resurrection.

IN SPECIAL DAYS

Mother's Day

Honor your father and your mother, so that your days may be long in the land that the Lord your God is giving you.

Exodus 20:12

In 1907 Anna Jarvis began a campaign to establish Mother's Day as a national holiday when she persuaded her mother's church to honor all mothers on the second anniversary of her mother's death. Her efforts intensified as she wrote letters to ministers, businessmen and politicians, until in 1914 President Woodrow Wilson proclaimed the second Sunday of May as Mother's Day.

We are grateful for all mothers who have faithfully provided for and nurtured their children. I thank God for a mother who was not only concerned about my physical and emotional needs, but also took seriously the promise she made at my baptism to lead me in the pathway of faith.

Caring, comforting, encouraging, and protecting are some of the attributes we ascribe to mothers. While we more commonly think of God in terms of being our Father, the Scriptures also have several references to God caring like a mother. An example portrays God as saying, "As a mother comforts her child, so I will comfort you" (Isaiah 66:13).

It is not easy to be a good mother, but mothers can turn to God as One who both exemplifies genuine love and caring, as well as promises strength, wisdom, guidance and compassion to fulfill

235

GLIMPSES OF GOD'S PRESENCE

the enormous responsibilities of the position. Drawing on God's abundant grace, mothers will learn to share grace with the precious ones entrusted to them. We can honor our mothers today through lives that show respect for the highest virtues they have taught us, and by lifting them up to God in prayer.

Blessings as you bring honor to your mother.

IN SPECIAL DAYS

Memorial Day

No one has greater love than this, to lay down one's life for one's friends.

John 15:13

More than two thousand flags blowing in the wind. Large flags... the size used to drape a coffin. Flags which have been given at the time of a funeral to families of veterans by a nation which is grateful for the military service rendered. Flags, each of which bears the name of the deceased veteran who is remembered. Flags which have been donated by the families to Fairmont Cemetery in Spokane, and are now flown each Memorial Day weekend at the cemetery. What a spectacular display!

Having been a teenager during World War II, I am impressed by the many striking stories which have been told about ordinary men and women involved in that war. I have been struck by how willingly so many of them went off to war. Many did not wait to be drafted, but lined up at the recruiting offices to volunteer to fight for freedom. They were willing to give up their lives, not only for their country, but to bring freedom to others. We owe them a real debt of gratitude. How can we ever really thank them?

There was another war and another volunteer–the one who spoke the words printed above. Jesus made the supreme sacrifice, and we are privileged to receive the gift of freedom and eternal life through him. How can we ever really thank him? The hymn writer responds, "Love so amazing, so divine, Demands my soul, my life, my all!"

Blessings as you rejoice in the gift of freedom won by others.

Father's Day

Children, obey your parents in the Lord, for this is right.

Ephesians. 6:1

We mark the third Sunday in June as a day to honor and give thanks for fathers. I have much reason to be grateful for my father. I remember him as a man of faith, integrity, honor and love. I have been blessed by his life.

Not every one has experienced a good relationship with their father. Very likely, Father's Day does not evoke positive and pleasant images for a person who has had an uncaring or abusive father, or one who did not provide a good example. Even under those circumstances a person can be thankful for the gift of life which came through father.

I am also grateful for another Father: the One we address as "Our Father" when we pray the Lord's Prayer. Hearing and reading his love letter to us we sense his amazing love and concern for his children, as well as his expectations of us. We learn about his dreams and hopes for us. As the realization of how good he is to us and how much he cares for us sinks in, we are dismayed by the ways we disappoint him. Yet he does not expel us from the family, but continually seeks to draw us into his loving embrace, offering full forgiveness through Jesus. We who hold the position of father can look to him to learn something of what it means to occupy the office.

IN SPECIAL DAYS

It is our custom to honor our fathers this Sunday with cards and gifts. It is our privilege to honor our fathers and our Father every day through lives of faith, integrity and love.

Blessings as you bring honor to your father (Father).

GLIMPSES OF GOD'S PRESENCE

Pentecost

*You will receive power when the Holy Spirit has
come upon you.*

Acts 1:8

Imagine hearing the roar of a mighty wind blowing in your house,
but your drapes are still hanging straight. Imagine seeing tongues
of fire along with the wind, but nothing in the house is burning. And then imagine that all the friends you had invited over
started speaking a variety of foreign languages. Amazed, bewil-
dered, perplexed, excited, confused and wondering are the words
used by various translations of Acts 2 to describe the reaction of
the people who observed such unusual happenings. Luke, the
author of Acts, wants us to know that God was doing another
of his great and amazing wonders in carrying out his plan of
salvation.

Pentecost is the third great festival of the Christian year. Christmas
is the festival of God the Father, Easter is the festival of God the
Son, and Pentecost is the festival celebrating the gift of God the
Holy Spirit. As the Holy Spirit came upon those followers of Jesus
on that Pentecost Day, they were inspired ("in-spirited") to boldly
proclaim the wonder of what God had done in Jesus. Those who
heard were likewise inspired, and multitudes became followers of
Jesus.

It is the Holy Spirit who points us to Jesus and draws us into a living relationship with God through Jesus, who calls us to be a part
of the people of God, the Holy Christian Church, and who enlight-

240

IN SPECIAL DAYS

ens and sanctifies us as we live as followers of Jesus. It is the Holy Spirit who dwells in us to produce the fruits of love, joy, peace, patience, kindness, goodness, faithfulness, gentleness, and self-control.

Blessings as you celebrate Pentecost Sunday.

GLIMPSES OF GOD'S PRESENCE

Independence Day (July 4)

Happy is the nation whose God is the Lord.
Psalm 33:12

The Fourth of July has become a special holiday in the United States as we commemorate the signing of the Declaration of Independence and the birthday of our nation. Have you ever wondered what happened to those men who signed that Declaration?

Five signers were captured by the British as traitors, and tortured before they died. Twelve had their homes ransacked and burned. Two lost their sons in the war, another had two sons captured. Nine of the 56 fought and died from wounds or hardships of the Revolutionary War. These were people who had income, money and property, but they were willing to sacrifice it all for the sake of liberty.

Today we are the beneficiaries of many who have made great sacrifices for the sake of liberty. Most of us will not be called upon to make such sacrifices, but we can express our gratitude by being renewers of the nation through our attitudes and behavior. Woodrow Wilson has written, "When I look back on the processes of history, when I survey the genesis of America, I see this written over every page: that the nations are renewed from the bottom, not from the top....A nation is as great, and only as great, as her rank and file....The hope of the United States in the present and in the future is the same that it has always been: it is the hope and the

242

IN SPECIAL DAYS

confidence that out of the unknown homes will come men who will constitute themselves the masters of industry and of politics."

Remember our nation in your prayers–and blessings as you celebrate Independence Day.

GLIMPSES OF GOD'S PRESENCE

Labor Day

*Happy is everyone who fears the Lord....You shall
eat the fruit of the labor of your hands.*

Psalm 128:1-2

Picture a loaf of bread in your hands. How did it get there? First, a farmer planted some seeds. On second thought, there were people involved before the farmer ever got the seed, including the geneticists who developed that particular variety of wheat, and people at the seed company who treated it to make it disease resistant. Later the fully developed heads of grain were harvested by the combine operator and hauled to the elevator by the truck driver where it was weighed and unloaded by the elevator crew. Then others took it to where it could be milled into flour. The flour was hauled to a bakery, where the baker created the loaf of bread, and put it in a wrapper. Other hands transported the loaf to the grocery store and put it on the shelf. You took it off the shelf, and paid the cashier.

And that is only part of the story. Think of the people who manufacture, transport and sell the farm machinery, the trucks, the milling machinery; produce and refine the fuel involved, make the bread wrapper possible, make the cash or credit card you use to pay for the bread, handle all the banking operations.

Labor Day provides an opportunity to be reminded of countless people who make our daily lives possible, and to thank God for the gift of people with a wide variety of abilities who work to serve us.

244

IN SPECIAL DAYS

It also provides an occasion to thank God for the gift of purposeful labor through which we are able to serve others.

Blessings as you rejoice in labor, and give thanks for laboring people.

GLIMPSES OF GOD'S PRESENCE

Reformation Day (October 31)

If you continue in my word, you are truly my disciples; and you will know the truth, and the truth will make you free.

John 8:31-32

The last Sunday in October has traditionally been observed among Lutheran churches as Reformation Sunday, in commemoration of the event which sparked the Reformation when, on October 31, 1517, Martin Luther nailed the ninety-five theses to the church door in Wittenberg, Germany. While the observation of Reformation Day points us back to a specific time in history, it is also a reminder that the Holy Spirit is continually at work, renewing and reforming his church, as well as the lives of individuals. Whatever denominational label we wear, we have reason to thank God for his ceaseless effort to preserve his people from false teachings, and enable them to be more faithful followers of Jesus.

It was though his study of the Scriptures that Martin Luther was led to become the leader of the sixteenth century Reformation movement. It was through a rekindled emphasis on biblical studies that remarkable changes in the Roman Catholic Church occurred in the middle of the last century. Numerous other awakenings have occurred through the centuries as Christians have been rooted in the Scriptures. The life of the church has truly been enriched as the followers of Jesus pay attention to the Word.

Blessings as you continue in his Word.

IN SPECIAL DAYS

All Saints Day (November 1)

To the church of God...to those who are sanctified in Christ Jesus, called to be saints, together with all those who in every place call on the name of our Lord Jesus Christ.

I Corinthians 1:2

Centuries ago the Church designated November 1 as a day to remember all the departed saints. We are grateful for the many people God raised up in a special way to proclaim the wondrous message of God's salvation in Jesus, to defend the church against heresy, and to be the loving presence of God in a needy world. We recall some names: Matthew, Mark, Luke, John, Peter, Paul, Augustine, Francis, and the list goes on.

I am reminded of what Martin Luther wrote about saints in one of his commentaries. When he was a monk he often wished he could see a saint, which he pictured as a super Christian who was not beset by sins the way the rest of us are. But later in life he was able to say that now he saw many saints; not the unreal saints he imagined before, but saints who, as followers of Jesus, were busy about the work God had given them in their daily lives.

The difference was that Luther had studied his Bible, and was letting the Bible rather than the church define what a saint is. The biblical picture is that a saint is one who is declared righteous and holy because of Jesus's righteousness and holiness. If we are

247

GLIMPSES OF GOD'S PRESENCE

among those who trust Jesus, we can put the word "saint" before our own name–saints in Jesus, though sinful in ourselves.

So, blessings on you, Saint (Your Name), as you strive to live as a follower of Jesus.

IN SPECIAL DAYS

Thanksgiving Day

*O give thanks to the Lord, for he is good; for his
steadfast love endures forever.*

Psalm 107:1

Dr. Alvin Rogness, President of Luther Seminary in the days I was a student there, has told two thanksgiving stories which I remember. The first was about a farmer who complained one year, "The potatoes are all so small they are good for nothing but to feed to the pigs." The next year he had an excellent crop of large, nicely shaped potatoes and complained, "There aren't any small ones to feed to the pigs." The second story was about an elderly, frail woman who had lost all but two of her teeth. With a smile she said, "I'm thankful they meet." Which of the two would you rather spend a Sunday afternoon with?

Most of us have a great deal to be thankful for. I have visited with many people who, while going through some real tragedies in their lives, impressed me by how often they commented, "When I look around and see others who are worse off, I am thankful I don't have to suffer more." While comparisons with others can often suggest reasons for giving thanks, the Scriptures suggest another powerful reason, God's amazing love and goodness which finds its most profound expression in Jesus.

We can give thanks today, not because we have plenty and have invested in the right stocks, but because in the midst of prosperity or poverty God is with us, calling us to remember who we truly are.

Blessings as all your thanksgiving is enriched by God's great love for you.

GLIMPSES OF GOD'S PRESENCE

St. Nicholas Day (December 6)

The righteous are generous and keep giving.
Psalm 37:21

December 6 is recognized as the day of commemoration of St. Nicholas, a fourth century bishop of Myra, in what is now known as Turkey. Nicholas is recognized for his great generosity, particularly toward children, the poor, and those in need. A legend about him concerned a family with three daughters who had plenty of suitors, but no dowry to make them eligible for marriage. When each of the older two daughters was of marriageable age, Nicholas anonymously put a bag of gold in the house so they could get married. While he was doing it for the third daughter, the father caught him in the act, thus discovering who the previously unknown benefactor was. As the father began to tell the story, others in the community realized from whom they had received unexpected gifts.

The feast of St. Nicholas was regularly celebrated in Holland where he was called Sinter Claus. The early Dutch settlers in New York brought the observance of the festival with them, and from them the tradition spread to other early Americans who were not aware of the fourth-century bishop, but liked the idea of Santa Claus.

Perhaps in the midst of this season, today is a good time to reflect on the spirit and the example of St. Nicholas, whose giving followed the pattern of his Lord in terms of his concern for the poor and needy.

Blessings as the spirit of St. Nicholas grows in you..

IN SPECIAL DAYS

Christmas Day

*And the Word became flesh and lived among us,
and we have seen his glory, the glory as of the
Father's only Son, full of grace and truth.*
John 1:14

Christmas enthralls us as we hear again the story of Jesus's birth in Bethlehem, with the attending angels' announcement to the shepherds, and the heavenly chorus singing praises to God. We have joyously sung the familiar carols inspired by the event. The story of the wise men following the star from the east to pay homage to the child has filled us with wonder.

In the Gospel according to John (1:1-18), we have a different slant on the Christmas story. There is no mention of the birth in a barn, visiting shepherds and wise men, or caroling angels. Rather, the focus is on what all this means as it is summed up in the verse printed above. Whenever I read this text those words jump out at me, calling me to stop and ponder the miracle and mystery of Christmas.

The Word became flesh and dwelt among us. I have always felt terribly inadequate as I have tried to write or preach about the statement. Perhaps the best we can do is simply pause and ponder the mystery:

. . .The Almighty Creator of the universe became a helpless baby.

. . .He who is spirit became flesh.

GLIMPSES OF GOD'S PRESENCE

. . .He, whom heaven and earth cannot contain, accepted the limitations of a human body.

. . .It was all inspired by God's tremendous love for us.

. . .What amazing grace!

Blessings as you ponder the Divine mystery.

IN SPECIAL DAYS

Birthday

You have been borne by me from your birth...even to your old age I am he, even when you turn gray I will carry you.

Isaiah 46:3-4

I enjoy seeing the excitement and anticipation of a five-year-old during the days leading up to the sixth birthday. It is a special day when the child will be the center of attention, have a party, and receive gifts. But the child will also be able to say, "I am six years old." The child feels there is a sense of accomplishment in becoming a year older.

I have seen some adults who have rather different feelings about birthdays. Aging is disturbing, and they resist revealing their age whenever possible. And yet, these same people do not wish that their time of having birthdays had come to an end.

Birthdays are a time to rejoice in and celebrate God's gift of life. We have reason to marvel at the mystery and the miracle of having been born with our own personal uniqueness. We consider the wonder of the cells of our body being formed into bones, muscles, tendons, brains, eyes, nerves, and blood. We stand in awe at how all this is put together in a way that gives each of us unique talents and aptitudes. What a marvel of creation!

Birthdays are a time to give thanks to God for his presence with us to keep this body, mind, and spirit functioning, and protected from all that has threatened it during the years. They are a time to

GLIMPSES OF GOD'S PRESENCE

give thanks for his abundant grace which has nurtured our spiritual life. Birthdays are also a time to look forward with hope, trusting the promise of God's steadfast love.

Blessings as you celebrate your birthday.

IN SPECIAL DAYS

Anniversary of a Baptism

*Go therefore and make disciples of all nations,
baptizing them in the name of the Father and of
the Son and of the Holy Spirit.*

Matthew 28:19

It was a simple, quiet, commonplace event. The sound of splashing water mingled with the words, "In the Name of the Father, and of the Son, and of the Holy Spirit." A towel dried the moistened head, and then the pastor's fingers made the sign of the cross on the forehead.

For all the simplicity, something profound happened as all the promises of God through the crucified and risen Jesus were enveloping the baptized one. The mystery of the washing of forgiveness, eternal life, adoption into the family of God, unity with Jesus in his crucifixion and resurrection, were somehow all being wrapped together with some water and some words. We can never understand, but we can marvel and stand in awe as the amazing love of God reaches out to enfold the newly baptized person.

Many of us may have forgotten the date of our baptism, and it slips by as any other ordinary day. But it is good if we can find some way to celebrate the day. If we celebrate Christmas, Easter, and Pentecost as days in which God has acted to bless the whole world, we can celebrate the anniversary of our baptism as a reminder that all of God's blessing of the world has reached out to touch us in a very personal way.

Blessings as you rejoice in your baptism.

GLIMPSES OF GOD'S PRESENCE

Wedding Anniversary

For this reason a man shall leave his father and mother and be joined to his wife, and the two shall become one flesh.

Matthew 19:5

When I answered the telephone I was surprised by the long distance call from a woman on the other side of the country as she expressed thanks for what I had said as I officiated at her wedding ten years earlier. She exclaimed, "What you told us is true. As we look back, we didn't really know what it meant to be in love at the time we were married, but we have been learning it through the years."

The couple was discovering the reality of their symbolic action at the wedding as they stepped forward to the altar, each taking an unlighted candle which they lit from the altar candle, then together lighting the unity candle, and placing their still burning candles on the altar. The individual candles represented them with all of the uniqueness of their personalities. They received their light from Christ, symbolized by the altar candle. Then together they committed themselves to the creation of a unity which took precedence over their individuality. God blessed their marriage, and they grew into that mysterious, miraculous, wonderful oneness which God promised as he gave the gift of marriage (Gen. 2:23, 24). Ten years later she was marveling at what had happened, and was continuing to happen.

IN SPECIAL DAYS

We know that marriages don't always reach the potential which God intends for them. But even in the difficult times of marriage, we can trust God's promise: "I will never leave you or forsake you" (Heb. 13:5).

Blessings as you rejoice in the oneness God has created for you.

GLIMPSES OF GOD'S PRESENCE

Anniversary of the Death of a Loved One

Blessed be the God and Father of our Lord Jesus Christ, the Father of mercies and the God of all consolation, who consoles us in all our affliction.
II Corinthians 1:3-4

The bounce had gone out of his step, and his shoulders drooped as he moved to the next task. Each task seemed more difficult now than previously. It was harder to concentrate, and errors became more frequent. The days were gloomy and the joy had gone out of living since his loved one had died. Could he ever adjust to the loss? Would there be any comfort?

A musical refrain began to repeat itself in his head. "Comfort ye, comfort ye my people....Comfort ye, comfort ye my people, says your God." Another biblical phrase was remembered: "God of all consolation." He was reminded of other passages which portrayed God as one who is concerned about his people in their needs and who holds them in his strong arms in their time of distress. The pain of the loss was not removed, but recalling the promises reminded him that he did not need to walk alone through his grief. He had a Father who also had experienced grief as the Son hung on the cross. That Father was with him now, and the gloom of the day was pierced by the light of God's love.

Losses come in a wide variety of forms as we journey through life. Every loss seems to take a bite out of us. In the midst of them we are encouraged to hold on to the promises of God, and know that we are never abandoned by him.

Blessings as you trust in God's presence every step along life's way.

258

Made in the USA